The Mythical Phaistos and Magliano Discs Decoded

CHRIS HEGG

Rowe Publishing

To all before me who showed me the way,

especially my grandfather,

who kindled the spark in my soul,

Richard Jack Hegg-

he now resides in Valhalla

as a true warrior.

ISBN: 978-1-64446-027-6

Visit the author's website for more information about his ongoing research, follow him on social media, sign up for his blog, and contact information for speaking arrangements.

AuthorChrisHegg.com

1 3 5 7 9 8 6 4 2

Printed in the United States of America
Published by

Rowe Publishing
www.rowepub.com

Contents

Comparison of the Magliano Disc Calendar to the Phaistos Disc Calendar

Previously, mostly concurrently, I deciphered the enigmatic Phaistos Disc as a related solar calendar to our modern calendar. Now it is absolute the two discs are related to each other, even with the fast time and distance, they correspond. Both relate directly to the Ancient Universal Language of petroglyphs, which I have deciphered a large portion of, especially dealing with the seasons and yearly calendar. The ancient language (over 12,500 years old) matches exactly to the ancient disc's segmentation and use.

The differences between the Phaistos Disc in relation to the Magliano Disc is the starting date. The Phaistos Disc begins on March 1st where the Magliano Disc begins on February 1st. Both contain a 24 month, 4 season divided solar calendar with prominent events listed such as equinoxes, solstices, seasons, and crossovers. Key marker symbols also define bracketed positions within the clocked symbol groups to align the calendars. Unique directions and carved spiral differences appear within the important times of the marked year to physically show connections to nature. See 2024 C Hegg report: The Phaistos Disc Artifact as the root design of the modern solar calendar, an early example of a bi-faced reproduction printing press template.[1]

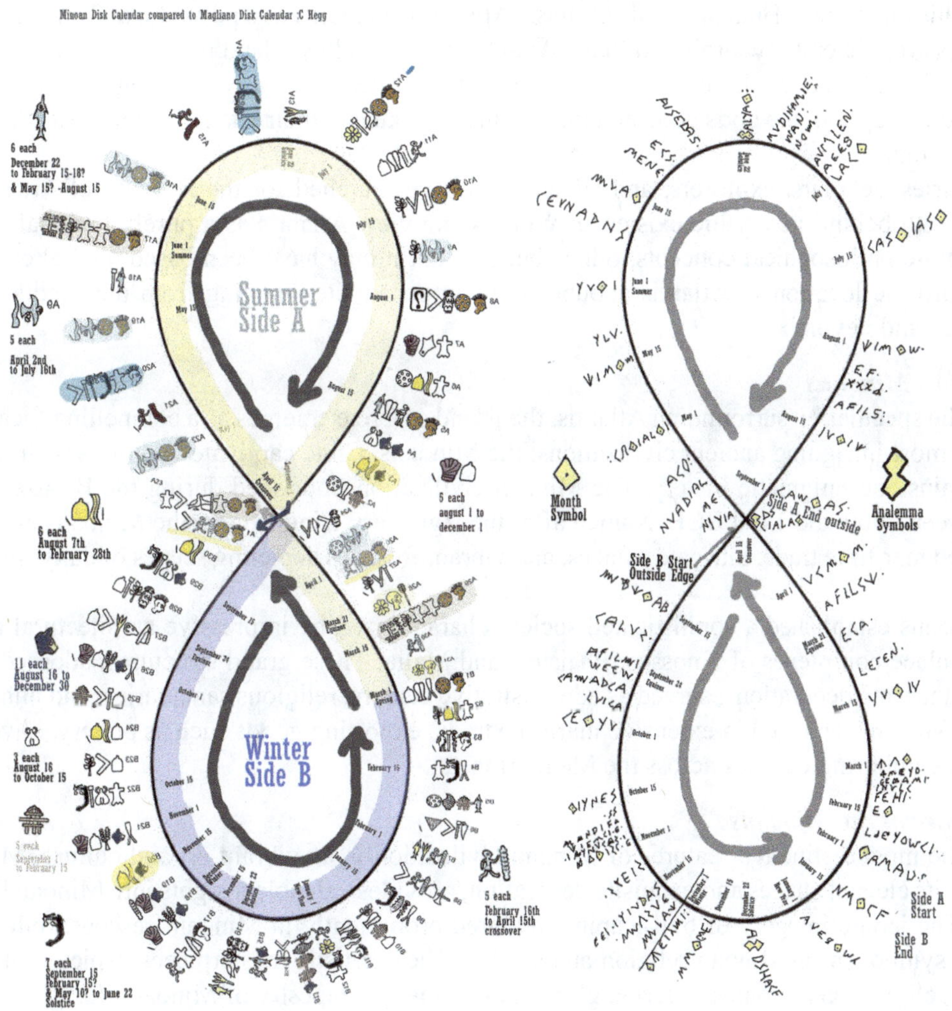

By author: a side-by-side comparison of both discs' calendar symbol groups around the solar analemma, Copyright 2024, free use if this report and the author's name are present with it.

The Enigma of Ancient Civilizations: Exploring Crete, Atlantis, and the Minoans

Ancient civilizations have long captured the imagination of historians, archaeologists, and enthusiasts alike. Among these civilizations, the Minoans of Crete stand out as a remarkable culture shrouded in mystery and intrigue. Their advanced society, vibrant art, and enigmatic disappearance have led some to speculate about their possible connection to the legendary lost city of Atlantis. In this chapter, we delve into the rich tapestry of ancient civilizations, focusing on the Minoans of Crete and their potential ties to the mythical Atlantis.

The Rise of Ancient Civilizations

The story of ancient civilizations begins thousands of years ago in the fertile river valleys of Mesopotamia, Egypt, the Indus Valley, and China. These early civilizations emerged as humans transitioned from nomadic hunter-gatherers to settled agricultural communities. With the development of agriculture came the growth of cities, writing systems, and complex social structures, laying the groundwork for the rise of civilization.

The Enigmatic Atlantis

At the heart of ancient mythology lies the enigmatic tale of Atlantis. Described by the ancient Greek philosopher Plato in his dialogues "Timaeus" and "Critias," Atlantis is depicted as a powerful and advanced civilization that met a catastrophic end. According to Plato, Atlantis was a wealthy island nation located beyond the Pillars of Hercules (often identified with the Strait of Gibraltar) and ruled by benevolent kings. However, due to their arrogance and corruption, the gods punished the Atlanteans, causing their island to sink beneath the waves in a single day and night.

For centuries, scholars, explorers, and adventurers have searched for the lost city of Atlantis, hoping to uncover the truth behind its mythic existence. While some view Atlantis as a purely fictional tale crafted by Plato to illustrate philosophical concepts, others believe that it may have been based on real events or places. Theories regard the location of Atlantis abound, with proposed sites ranging from the Mediterranean to the Atlantic Ocean and beyond.

The Mysterious Minoans

Amidst the speculation surrounding Atlantis, the island of Crete emerges as a compelling focal point. Home to one of the most intriguing ancient civilizations, the Minoans, Crete captivates scholars with its rich archaeological remains and enigmatic history. The Minoan civilization flourished during the Bronze Age, reaching its peak between 2000 and 1450 BCE. Named after the legendary King Minos, the Minoans are renowned for their advanced maritime trade, intricate palaces, and vibrant frescoes depicting scenes of daily life and religious rituals.

The Minoans established a sophisticated society characterized by impressive architectural achievements, such as the palace complexes of Knossos, Phaistos, and Malia. These grand structures, adorned with colorful frescoes and intricate decorations, served as administrative centers, religious sanctuaries, and hubs of economic activity. The Minoans engaged in extensive maritime trade, exporting goods such as pottery, olive oil, and luxury items to neighboring cultures across the Mediterranean.

Art and Culture of the Minoans

One of the most distinctive features of Minoan civilization is its vibrant art and culture. Minoan pottery, renowned for its elegant shapes and exquisite decoration, provides valuable insights into Minoan life and artistic expression. The iconic imagery of bull-leaping, featured prominently in Minoan frescoes, reflects the importance of bull symbolism in Minoan religion and society. These artistic masterpieces depict scenes of feasting, dancing, and religious ceremonies, offering glimpses into the rich tapestry of Minoan life.

The Decline of Minoan Civilization

Despite their achievements, the Minoans faced challenges that ultimately led to their decline. Around 1450 BCE, the island of Thera (modern-day Santorini) was rocked by a massive volcanic eruption, triggering tsunamis and ashfall that devastated nearby settlements, including Crete. Some scholars speculate that this cataclysmic event may have dealt a severe blow to Minoan civilization, contributing to its eventual downfall.

The Minoans and Atlantis: A Connection?

The parallels between Minoan civilization and the descriptions of Atlantis in Plato's dialogues have led some to speculate about a possible connection between the two. Proponents of this theory point to similarities in architectural styles, maritime prowess, and cultural achievements shared by both civilizations. Additionally, the geographic location of Crete, situated in the Eastern Mediterranean between Europe, Asia, and Africa, aligns with Plato's description of Atlantis as a maritime power that controlled trade routes in the ancient world.

The Enigma of the Phaistos Disc: A Journey into Ancient Mysteries

The Phaistos Disc stands as one of the most intriguing artifacts from the ancient world, captivating scholars and enthusiasts with its enigmatic symbols and mysterious origin. Discovered on the island of Crete, the Phaistos Disc continues to puzzle researchers, sparking numerous theories about its purpose and meaning. In this chapter, we embark on a journey to explore the Phaistos Disc, delving into its discovery, unique characteristics, and myriad theories proposed by scholars over the years.

Discovery of the Phaistos Disc

The story of the Phaistos Disc begins in 1908 when Italian archaeologist Luigi Pernier unearthed the artifact during excavations at the Minoan palace of Phaistos (also spelled Phaestos or Festos) in southern Crete. Carved from clay and measuring approximately 15 centimeters in diameter, the disc features a series of stamped hieroglyphic symbols arranged in a spiral pattern on both sides. Its discovery within a Minoan context, alongside other artifacts dating to the second millennium BCE, firmly places the Phaistos Disc within the timeframe of the Minoan civilization.

Unique Characteristics of the Phaistos Disc

What sets the Phaistos Disc apart from other ancient artifacts is its intricate design and the mysterious symbols adorning its surface. The disc contains a total of 241 symbols, divided into 61 groups, arranged in a spiral pattern that begins at the disc's outer edge and spirals inward toward the center. The symbols themselves are stamped or imprinted onto the clay surface, rather than being incised or engraved, indicating a unique method of production. Furthermore, no other examples of similar discs or inscriptions have been found elsewhere in the archaeological record, adding to the disc's mystique.

Theories Regarding the Purpose and Meaning of the Phaistos Disc

Since its discovery over a century ago, the Phaistos Disc has sparked a wide range of theories regarding its purpose and meaning. Scholars from various disciplines, including archaeology, linguistics, and cryptography, have offered interpretations based on linguistic analysis, comparative studies, and technological advancements. Some of the most prominent theories include:

1. Religious or Ritualistic Artifact: One theory posits that the Phaistos Disc served a religious or ritualistic purpose within Minoan society. Advocates of this theory suggest that the symbols may represent sacred symbols, religious concepts, or ritual formulas associated with Minoan religious practices. However, the exact nature of these rituals remains speculative, as no direct evidence has been uncovered to support this interpretation.

2. Calendar or Astronomical Device: Another hypothesis proposes that the Phaistos Disc functioned as a calendar or astronomical device, encoding information related to lunar phases, celestial events, or agricultural cycles. Proponents of this theory point to the spiral layout of the symbols and their potential

alignment with astronomical phenomena. However, the lack of clear astronomical references and the complexity of the symbols make this interpretation challenging to verify.

3. Writing System or Language: Perhaps the most debated theory revolves around the idea that the symbols on the Phaistos Disc represent a writing system or language used by the Minoans. Scholars have attempted to decipher the symbols using comparative linguistics, phonetic analysis, and statistical methods. While some proposed decipherments have claimed to identify the language of the disc, such as a form of ancient Greek or a unique Minoan script, these interpretations remain highly speculative and controversial.

4. Artistic or Decorative Artifact: Alternatively, some researchers suggest that the Phaistos Disc may have served a purely artistic or decorative function, devoid of any specific meaning or linguistic content. According to this view, the symbols on the disc may represent abstract designs, patterns, or decorative motifs commonly found in Minoan art. However, this interpretation fails to account for the deliberate arrangement of the symbols in a spiral pattern and the absence of similar artifacts in the archaeological record.

Deciphering the Past: Exploring Ancient Writing Systems

Writing is a remarkable human invention that has played a pivotal role in the development and transmission of culture, knowledge, and history. Throughout the ancient world, diverse civilizations devised unique writing systems to record their languages, beliefs, and achievements. In this chapter, we embark on a journey through time to explore the evolution of ancient writing systems, from the earliest pictographic symbols to the sophisticated scripts of ancient civilizations such as cuneiform, hieroglyphics, Linear A, and Linear B. We will delve into the significance of these writing systems in understanding ancient civilizations, the challenges of deciphering them, and the breakthroughs that have illuminated the past.

Cuneiform: The Script of Mesopotamia

One of the oldest known writing systems, cuneiform, emerged in ancient Mesopotamia around 3500 BCE. Developed by the Sumerians, cuneiform initially consisted of pictographic symbols representing objects and concepts, which evolved into a complex system of wedge-shaped characters inscribed on clay tablets. Cuneiform was used to record administrative, legal, and religious texts, providing invaluable insights into the social, political, and economic life of Mesopotamian societies such as Sumer, Akkad, and Babylon.

Deciphering cuneiform posed significant challenges to scholars due to the script's intricate nature and the vast corpus of texts written in multiple languages and dialects. However, breakthroughs in the 19th and 20th centuries, such as the discovery of the Behistun Inscription and the Rosetta Stone, enabled researchers to unlock the secrets of cuneiform by comparing known languages with unknown scripts, paving the way for the decipherment of ancient languages like Sumerian, Akkadian, and Hittite.

Hieroglyphics: The Sacred Script of Egypt

In ancient Egypt, hieroglyphics served as the sacred script used for religious inscriptions, monumental carvings, and royal decrees. Hieroglyphic writing combined pictorial symbols, phonetic signs, and determinatives to convey meaning, reflecting the complex religious beliefs and cosmology of Egyptian civilization. The decipherment of hieroglyphics remained a mystery for centuries until the discovery of the Rosetta Stone in 1799, which contained a decree written in three scripts: hieroglyphics, demotic, and Greek. The breakthrough came in 1822 when French scholar Jean-François Champollion successfully deciphered the hieroglyphic script by comparing it with the Greek text, unlocking the secrets of ancient Egyptian civilization.

Linear A and Linear B: Scripts of the Aegean Bronze Age

During the Aegean Bronze Age, two distinct writing systems, Linear A and Linear B, emerged on the islands of Crete and mainland Greece, respectively. Linear A, associated with the Minoan civilization of Crete, remains undeciphered to this day, hindering our understanding of Minoan language and culture. Linear B, on the other hand, was used by the Mycenaean Greeks to record administrative and economic texts on clay tablets. The decipherment of Linear B in the mid-20th century by architect and amateur linguist Michael Ventris revealed the earliest known form of Greek, shedding light on Mycenaean society and its connections with the wider Mediterranean world.

Challenges of Decipherment

Deciphering ancient writing systems poses numerous challenges to scholars, including the absence of bilingual texts, the loss of linguistic continuity, and the limited understanding of the cultural context in which the scripts were used. Additionally, many ancient scripts exhibit complex morphological and grammatical features, making it difficult to identify individual signs and decipher their meanings. Furthermore, the incomplete nature of archaeological finds and the fragility of writing materials present obstacles to the preservation and interpretation of ancient texts.

Breakthroughs and Insights

Despite these challenges, breakthroughs in decipherment have revolutionized our understanding of ancient civilizations, providing invaluable insights into their languages, cultures, and histories. The decipherment of cuneiform, hieroglyphics, Linear A, and Linear B has unlocked a wealth of knowledge about Mesopotamia, Egypt, Crete, and Mycenaean Greece, revealing the complexities of ancient societies and their contributions to human civilization. Through interdisciplinary research and collaboration, scholars continue to push the boundaries of decipherment, unraveling the mysteries of the past and preserving the legacy of ancient writing systems for future generations.

Unlocking Secrets: An Exploration of Cryptography and Codebreaking

Cryptography, the art and science of secret writing, has played a pivotal role throughout history, from ancient civilizations to the modern era. Cryptography encompasses the methods used to conceal information through encryption, as well as the techniques employed to decipher encrypted messages through codebreaking or cryptanalysis. In this chapter, we embark on a journey through the fascinating world of cryptography and codebreaking, exploring its history, techniques, and notable examples of cryptanalysis that have shaped the course of human events.

Ancient Methods of Encryption

The origins of cryptography can be traced back to ancient civilizations, where rulers, generals, and diplomats employed various methods to protect sensitive information from prying eyes. One of the earliest known examples of encryption is the use of simple substitution ciphers by the ancient Greeks and Romans, where letters of the alphabet are replaced with other letters or symbols according to a predetermined key. Another ancient method of encryption is steganography, the practice of concealing secret messages within innocent-looking texts or images.

Famous Examples of Cryptanalysis

Throughout history, cryptanalysis has played a crucial role in uncovering hidden messages and unraveling the secrets of encrypted communications. One of the most famous examples of cryptanalysis is the decipherment of the Rosetta Stone in 1822 by French scholar Jean-François Champollion. The Rosetta Stone, a slab of black basalt inscribed with a decree in three scripts—hieroglyphics, demotic, and Greek—provided the key to unlocking the mysteries of ancient Egyptian hieroglyphics, allowing Champollion to decipher the script and decipher the language.

Another enigmatic example of cryptanalysis is the Voynich manuscript, a mysterious book written in an unknown script and language, dating to the 15th century. For centuries, scholars and cryptographers have attempted to decipher the Voynich manuscript, but its contents remain an unsolved puzzle to this day. Despite numerous theories and conjectures, the true meaning and purpose of the manuscript continue to elude researchers, fueling speculation and fascination with its cryptic contents.

Modern Cryptography and Codebreaking Techniques

In the modern era, cryptography has evolved into a sophisticated science, with applications ranging from secure communication and data encryption to cybersecurity and computer algorithms. Modern cryptographic techniques include symmetric encryption, where a single key is used for both encryption and decryption, and asymmetric encryption, where separate keys are used for encryption and decryption. Cryptography also encompasses the field of cryptanalysis, which employs mathematical algorithms, statistical methods, and computational techniques to break encrypted messages and uncover hidden information.

Famous examples of modern codebreaking include the efforts of British cryptanalysts during World War II to decipher the German Enigma machine, a complex electromechanical device used by the Nazis to encrypt military communications. The successful decryption of the Enigma code by British codebreakers at Bletchley Park, including mathematician Alan Turing, played a crucial role in Allied victory and significantly shortened the duration of the war.

The Quest for Ancient Scripts and Undeciphered Languages

Throughout history, humanity has been captivated by the allure of lost languages and undeciphered scripts, viewing them as tantalizing puzzles waiting to be solved. From the mythical Tower of Babel to the enigmatic Linear A and the Indus Valley script, the quest to unlock the secrets of ancient languages has fueled the imagination of scholars, linguists, and enthusiasts alike. In this chapter, we embark on a journey through the ages, exploring the fascination with lost languages, the methodologies employed in deciphering ancient scripts, and the challenges that arise in unraveling the mysteries of the past.

The Myth of the Tower of Babel

The story of the Tower of Babel, found in the Book of Genesis, recounts the tale of a mythical tower built by humanity to reach the heavens. In response to their arrogance, God confounds their language, causing confusion and scatters the people across the Earth. While the Tower of Babel myth serves as a religious allegory, it also reflects humanity's enduring fascination with language and its power to unite or divide communities.

Ancient Scripts: The Legacy of Lost Civilizations

The ancient world was home to a diverse array of writing systems, each reflecting the unique cultures and civilizations that created them. From the hieroglyphics of ancient Egypt to the cuneiform script of Mesopotamia, these ancient scripts served as tools for communication, record-keeping, and cultural expression. However, with the passage of time, many of these scripts fell out of use, leaving behind inscriptions and texts that remained undeciphered for centuries.

Linear A: The Mysterious Script of the Minoans

Among the most tantalizing examples of undeciphered scripts is Linear A, the writing system used by the Minoan civilization of ancient Crete. Dating to the second millennium BCE, Linear A remains a mystery to scholars, who have yet to decipher its symbols and unlock the language it represents. Despite extensive efforts and numerous theories, Linear A continues to elude decipherment, leaving unanswered questions about Minoan culture, religion, and trade.

The Indus Valley Script: An Enigma of Ancient India

Similarly enigmatic is the script of the Indus Valley civilization, one of the earliest urban civilizations in ancient India. Dating back to the third millennium BCE, the Indus Valley script is found on seals, pottery, and other artifacts excavated from archaeological sites such as Harappa and Mohenjo-Daro. Despite decades of research and speculation, the Indus Valley script remains undeciphered, hindering our understanding of this ancient civilization and its language.

Methodologies in Deciphering Ancient Scripts

Deciphering ancient scripts requires a multidisciplinary approach that combines linguistic analysis, comparative studies, and archaeological evidence. Linguists study the structure and grammar of the script, looking for patterns and recurring symbols that may indicate phonetic or semantic values. Comparative studies involve comparing the undeciphered script with known languages or scripts, searching for similarities or borrowed elements that may provide clues to its meaning. Archaeological evidence, such as inscriptions, artifacts, and cultural contexts, can also offer valuable insights into the language and culture associated with the script.

Challenges in Deciphering Ancient Languages

Deciphering ancient scripts presents numerous challenges to scholars, including the lack of bilingual texts or Rosetta Stone-like inscriptions, the absence of a known linguistic context, and the limitations of archaeological evidence. Additionally, ancient scripts may exhibit complex morphological and grammatical features that defy straightforward interpretation, further complicating the decipherment process. Furthermore, the erosion of inscriptions over time and the loss of linguistic continuity pose obstacles to understanding the script's original meaning and purpose.

Breakthroughs and Future Prospects

Despite these challenges, breakthroughs in decipherment have been achieved through persistence, collaboration, and advances in technology. The successful decipherment of scripts such as Linear B and the Mayan hieroglyphics demonstrates the potential for unlocking the secrets of ancient languages with innovative methodologies and interdisciplinary approaches. Furthermore, ongoing research and new discoveries continue to shed light on previously unknown scripts and languages, offering hope for future breakthroughs in decipherment and a deeper understanding of humanity's linguistic heritage.

Ancient Knowledge of Celestial Movements and the Solar Analemma

The analemma, a figure-eight-shaped curve that represents the apparent motion of the Sun in the sky over the course of a year, is a testament to the profound understanding of celestial phenomena held by ancient cultures. While the analemma may appear as a modern scientific concept, its roots can be traced back to ancient civilizations that observed and recorded the movements of the Sun with remarkable precision. In this chapter, we explore the analemma and the knowledge of celestial movements possessed by ancient peoples, shedding light on their sophisticated understanding of astronomy and its significance in their cultures.

Ancient Observations of Celestial Phenomena

Ancient civilizations such as the Egyptians, Babylonians, Greeks, and Mayans were keen observers of the heavens, studying the movements of the Sun, Moon, planets, and stars to track time, predict seasons, and determine agricultural cycles. Through careful observation and empirical measurements, these cultures developed sophisticated astronomical calendars and systems of reckoning that allowed them to synchronize their societies with the rhythms of the cosmos.

The Analemma in Ancient Cultures

While the term "analemma" may not have been used by ancient cultures, the concept of the Sun's apparent motion along a figure-eight path in the sky was well understood and incorporated into their calendars and cosmological beliefs. For example, in ancient Egypt, the annual flooding of the Nile River was closely tied to the heliacal rising of the star Sirius, which was observed and recorded with great accuracy. Similarly, in ancient Mesopotamia, the movements of celestial bodies were meticulously documented on clay tablets, allowing astronomers to predict celestial events and agricultural cycles.

The Greeks, with their advanced knowledge of mathematics and astronomy, also recognized the cyclical nature of the Sun's apparent motion and its significance in determining the length of the solar year. Greek astronomers such as Hipparchus and Ptolemy made detailed observations of the Sun's position in the sky and developed mathematical models to describe its apparent motion, laying the groundwork for modern methods of celestial navigation and timekeeping.

The Mayans, renowned for their complex calendrical systems and astronomical achievements, also incorporated the analemma into their calendars and religious rituals. The Mayan Long Count calendar, which tracks the passage of time in units of days, years, and baktuns (periods of approximately 394 years), was based on precise astronomical observations of celestial phenomena, including the Sun's annual journey along the analemma.

Interpreting the Analemma: Symbolism and Cosmology

In addition to its practical utility in timekeeping and calendar reckoning, the analemma held symbolic significance in many ancient cultures, representing the cyclical nature of life, death, and rebirth. In Egyptian cosmology, for example, the Sun god Ra was believed to traverse the heavens in a solar barque, symbolizing the journey of the Sun along its analemma-shaped path. Similarly, in Mayan cosmology, the analemma was associated with the god Kukulkan, depicted as a feathered serpent symbolizing the Sun's passage through the sky.

The analemma also played a central role in religious rituals and ceremonies, serving as a marker for important celestial events such as solstices, equinoxes, and eclipses. Temples and observatories aligned with the movements of the Sun and other celestial bodies were constructed by ancient cultures to facilitate the observation of these events and the performance of associated rituals.

The Study of Petroglyphs and Their Myth by Modern Archaeologists

Petroglyphs, ancient rock engravings and carvings, provide a window into the beliefs, experiences, and artistic expressions of past cultures. These remarkable works of art, etched onto the surfaces of cliffs, boulders, and cave walls, have fascinated archaeologists for centuries, offering valuable insights into the lives and cultures of the people who created them. In this chapter, we explore the study of petroglyphs by archaeologists, examining their methods, interpretations, and significance in understanding ancient societies.

Discovery and Documentation

The discovery and documentation of petroglyphs often begin with field surveys conducted by archaeologists and researchers. These surveys involve systematically exploring areas known for their rock art, such as deserts, canyons, and coastal cliffs, in search of new sites and previously undocumented petroglyphs. Once discovered, petroglyphs are carefully documented using a variety of techniques, including photography, sketching, and 3D laser scanning, to create detailed records of their size, location, and surrounding environment.

Interpretation and Analysis

Interpreting the meaning and significance of petroglyphs is complex. All motifs, symbols, and stylistic elements present in petroglyphs to identify recurring patterns, themes, and cultural motifs. Comparative studies with other forms of material culture, such as pottery, tools, and architecture, can provide additional context for understanding the cultural and temporal significance of petroglyphs within a broader archaeological framework.

Dating and Chronology

Establishing the age and chronology of petroglyphs is essential for understanding their cultural context and significance. Archaeologists use a variety of dating techniques, including radiocarbon dating, thermoluminescence dating, and stylistic analysis, to determine the age of petroglyphs and their associated archaeological deposits. By correlating the chronological sequence of petroglyphs with other forms of archaeological evidence, such as pottery styles and settlement patterns, researchers can reconstruct the cultural and historical context in which the petroglyphs were created.

Regional and Cultural Variability

Petroglyphs exhibit a remarkable diversity of styles, motifs, and themes that reflect the cultural, environmental, and historical contexts of the societies that created them. From the intricate geometric patterns of the Southwestern United States to the vivid depictions of animals and hunting scenes in the Sahara Desert, petroglyphs offer unique insights into the beliefs, practices, and lifeways of ancient cultures around the world. Regional studies of petroglyphs allow archaeologists to identify patterns of cultural continuity and change over time, as well as connections between different societies and regions.

Symbolism and Meaning

The interpretation of petroglyphs involves unraveling the symbolism and meaning encoded within their images and motifs. Many petroglyphs depict animals, humans, celestial bodies, and geometric patterns that are laden with symbolic significance and cultural meaning. For example, animal motifs may represent totemic symbols, clan identities, or hunting rituals, while geometric patterns may convey concepts of cosmic order, fertility, or shamanic visions. By studying the cultural context and ethnographic parallels, archaeologists can decipher the symbolic language of petroglyphs and reconstruct the worldview of the societies that created them.

Preservation and Conservation

Preserving and protecting petroglyphs is essential for ensuring their survival for future generations. Archaeologists work closely with local communities, government agencies, and conservation organizations to develop strategies for managing and safeguarding petroglyph sites from threats such as vandalism, looting, erosion, and development. Techniques such as rock shelter stabilization, site monitoring, and public education programs help raise awareness of the importance of preserving these invaluable cultural treasures.

Exploring Theories of Prehistoric Oceanic Travel and Global Languages

The study of ancient seafaring and the possibility of global languages in prehistoric times have long captivated both mainstream scholars and fringe theorists. While traditional archaeology relies on empirical evidence and written records to reconstruct ancient maritime routes and linguistic developments, fringe science often explores speculative theories based on mythology, folklore, and anomalous archaeological finds. In this chapter, we delve into the diverse theories proposed by both mainstream and fringe researchers regarding how ancient peoples may have navigated the seas and potentially communicated in a global language before written records.

Mainstream Theories of Prehistoric Oceanic Travel

Mainstream archaeology acknowledges that ancient peoples were capable mariners who navigated the seas using rudimentary navigational techniques such as celestial navigation, coastal landmarks, and currents. Evidence of ancient maritime trade networks and seafaring cultures, such as the Phoenicians, Polynesians, and Vikings, supports the notion that humans have been traversing the oceans for thousands of years. Moreover, the discovery of ancient seafaring vessels, harbor sites, and navigational tools provides tangible evidence of prehistoric oceanic travel.

One prominent theory proposed by mainstream scholars is the "Out of Africa" hypothesis, which posits that early human migrations out of Africa spread across land bridges and coastal routes to populate distant continents. Coastal migrations along coastlines and river systems, such as the migration of Homo sapiens into Southeast Asia and Australia, suggest that ancient peoples were adept at utilizing maritime resources for exploration and colonization.

Fringe Theories of Ancient Oceanic Travel

Fringe theorists often speculate on more controversial and unconventional theories of ancient oceanic travel, drawing upon mythology, ancient texts, and anomalous archaeological finds to support their claims. Some fringe researchers propose that advanced ancient civilizations, such as Atlantis or Mu, possessed sophisticated seafaring technologies and navigational knowledge that allowed them to traverse the oceans and establish global maritime networks.

Other fringe theories suggest that ancient peoples may have utilized unconventional methods of navigation, such as ley lines, magnetic anomalies, or even extraterrestrial guidance to navigate the seas. These theories often draw upon anecdotal evidence, speculative interpretations of ancient texts, and alleged archaeological discoveries to support their claims, but are typically dismissed by mainstream scholars due to a lack of empirical evidence and methodological rigor.

The Search for a Global Language

In addition to theories of ancient oceanic travel, fringe researchers have also proposed the existence of a global language spoken by ancient civilizations before written records. Proponents of this idea point to linguistic similarities and shared vocabulary among disparate cultures as evidence of a common ancestral language spoken by ancient seafarers.

One popular theory, known as "Proto-World" or "Nostratic," posits that all human languages share a common linguistic root that originated in a single ancestral language spoken by early human populations. While mainstream linguistics acknowledges the existence of language families and linguistic relatedness, the notion of a single global language spoken by ancient peoples remains speculative and controversial within academic circles.

Decryption Report on Phaistos Disc Submitted by Author 2024

The Phaistos Disc Artifact as the root design of the modern solar calendar, an early example of a bi-faced reproduction printing press template.

January 2024 White Paper by
Chris Hegg
Independent Researcher
chrishegg@hotmail.com

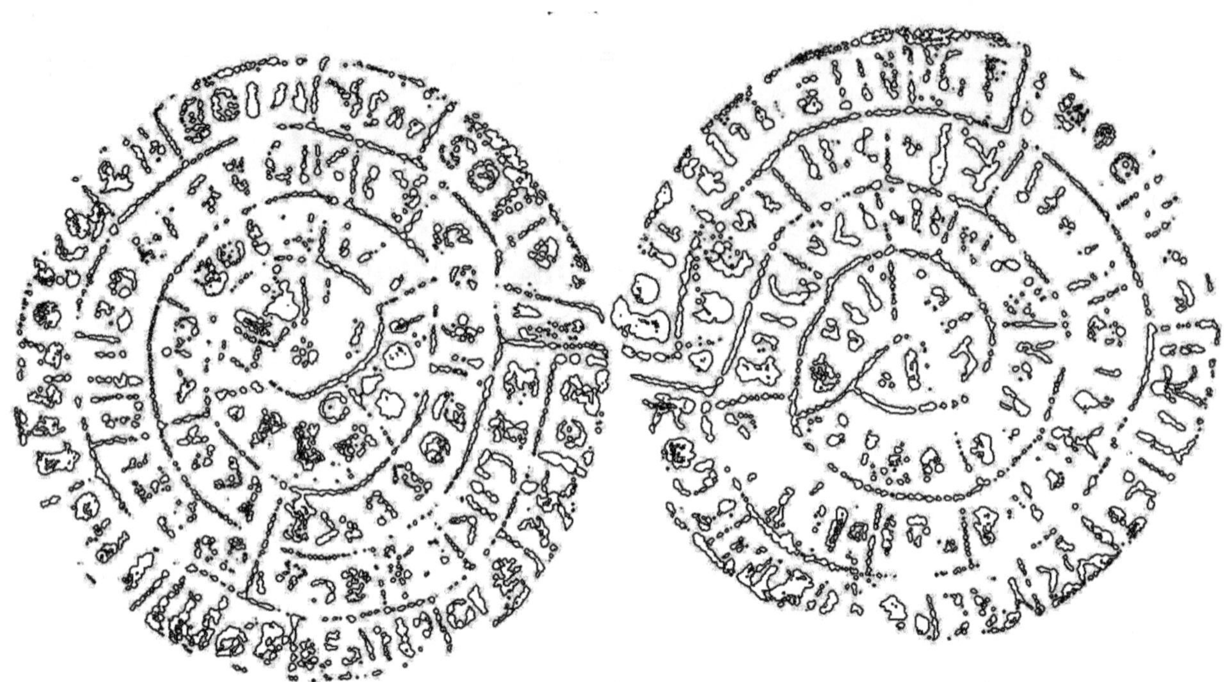

Photo representation of an ink-stamped copy on paper from clay stamps generated from the Phaistos Disc template to show the detail possible with such a technique. This was generated using a lower-standard museum replica that had far less descriptive carved markings. By Author 2023

Decryption Report on Phaistos Disc Introduction

The Phaistos Disc is the earliest known example of a fully formed solar calendar and a possible origin of the modern calendar. The Phaistos Disc is a bi-faced template for reproducing clay imprints to use as ink printing dies/stamps. The Phaistos Disc is possibly the first printing press template.

The design on the two-sided disc produces a divided rendition of a balanced version of the solar calendar year, with a foundational spiral configuration used in the Ancient Universal Language (C Hegg, 2017 Ancient Universal Language of Man).

The disc's calendar year is divided into two seasons, Summer and Winter, with seasons beginning on the first day of the month of equinoxes and solstices.

The summer section is on Side A and comprises from March 1st to the ending symbol group of September 1st, which is just days away from the second crossover of the solar analemma.

The disc's Side B starts the winter section begins at the second crossover of the solar analemma and ends with the listed symbol group of March 1st.

The disc is meant to be read from the central point on each side, outward around the edge, to the ending marks of the five dots. The month count is twenty-four. Divisions are listed for solstices, equinoxes, crossovers, new year, and all four seasons, with two per side. Other important holidays, such as Imbolc on February 1st, are also listed.

Some sections of the calendar are perfectly tuned and provide a solid foundation for the displaying of a well-defined year. The summer section on Side A represents a perfectly tuned following of the analemma and seems to hold roots in a long history of usage. Side B begins to show unusual changes in symbol types and groupings that are not as defined and appear to be a newer addition to the calendar. The best-represented homogenous symbology seems to be from September to the new year. It appears to have some rationale that indicates it will be used longer than the January and February months. It seems the most unique and maybe the most experimental months were added between January and March. These four months have the least cohesive arrangements for decipherment.

Another important observation is the association with similar-type symbols that have the potential to be related in use/meaning to one another. For instance, the walking man symbol and the standing man symbol or shackled man symbol. All plant symbols may relate to the seed-sowing symbol and so forth. **Slight nuances in design changes, such as bare stick symbols to full-growth plant symbols, are crucial to understanding reasoning toward these groups.**

Discussed later are the slight tail marks seen on and off of certain symbols, such as the helmet symbol. The author is very confident (again using the Ancient Universal Language template) that the tail symbols are, in at least some instances but probably all, the rendition of 'shadow' and thus cast a shadow or run beyond the symbol's shadow in relation to likely awaiting an upcoming event of the season. The actual use in its most basic form means to stand still as one 'casts his own shadow' while stagnant.

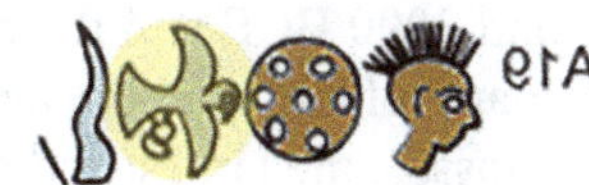

*Slight differences denote meaning

Author rendition showing how slight variations change meaning, such as the very similar symbol groups of May 1, May 15, and June 15 months of a forward bird, backward bird, and feet added to the horn symbol of the June 15 group.

Author Background

C Hegg, the author, conducts independent research on ancient enigmas, primarily within his home country of the United States, where one can travel to many locations. He became fascinated with the Phaistos Disc and has studied it for many decades on and off. He realized that the disc was unique compared to the ancient language witnessed on petroglyph panels throughout the world but it maintained the core fundamentals of the language. Thus began his realization that he would have to dedicate a great deal of time to deciphering the disc if he were to prove the usage of the device, and thus, the existence of a universal language.

As the disc is highly modified from the base language (a symbolic language based predominantly on natural events and cycles), it took a long time to crack the specific usage of this device. It took a long time to research the ancient Greek region of influence before he was able to finally find the keys needed to impart specific times and clocking of the device to understand its usage correctly. It was this breakthrough that verified his initial observation that the disc's true purpose was sound. And in the end, his clocking of the symbols was one whole season off from his initial thought. But even then, the complex nature of the groups and high count proved challenging to discover the final positions, only three positions off from his second attempted pattern.

As an independent researcher, Hegg has published several books on the topic of petroglyphs (rock art) as an ancient language. In his 2017 book *Ancient Universal Language of Man*, he references many archaic devices, megalithic sites, and other various artifacts, along with global renditions of petroglyphs, pictographs, and geoglyphs/intaglios. In this book, he references the Phaistos Disc, described as an ancient printing press device for reproducible images of the solar calendar, as it was based on the Universal Language Symbol System. Hegg has been unable to follow up on the publication and decipherment until now.

There is little interest or competence present in deciphering ancient languages beyond symbological constraints. Thus, present here is a systematic breakdown of the Phaistos Disc symbology as it relates to the connection to the solar analemma. Ignored are the definitions and meanings of the symbol groups, other than how they might connect to the location on the calendar precisely.

It is hoped someone else who is driven to discover the language can further define its meaning from this report. It appears, however, that there are essential precessions, divisions, celebrations, and naturally connected events that are locked within the symbol groups as they relate to the different seasons. This report will attempt to flesh out these occurrences. Some general descriptive meanings will be employed that have come up in Hegg's research of the area, as well as known regional thinking at times when it is believed such evidence has substance.

The Island of Crete, Greece

The island of Crete, situated in the eastern Mediterranean Sea, holds a unique place as a cradle of civilization. With many cultures spanning millennia, Crete's strategic location at the crossroads of Europe, Asia, and Africa enabled the rise and flourishing of remarkable civilizations from the Minoans to the Mycenaeans, and later from Rome, Byzantium, Venice, and the Ottomans.

At the heart of Crete's ancient heritage lies the Minoan civilization, which emerged during the Bronze Age around 3000 BCE and flourished until approximately 1100 BCE. Named after the legendary King Minos, the Minoans left an indelible mark, characterized by palaces, frescoes, and advanced engineering feats. The Palace of Knossos, the largest and most famous of Minoan palaces, stands as a testament to their architectural prowess and organizational sophistication. These palaces served as centers of administration, trade, and religious rituals, reflecting the Minoans' complex social structure and maritime prowess.

The Minoans were adept sailors and traders, dominating the Aegean Sea and establishing extensive commercial networks that stretched as far as Egypt, Anatolia, and the Levant. Their maritime supremacy and cultural influence are evident in the widespread distribution of Minoan artifacts and artistic motifs throughout the Mediterranean world.

However, the decline of the Minoan civilization remains shrouded in mystery, with theories ranging from natural disasters, such as the eruption of Thera (modern-day Santorini), to invasion and internal unrest. The vacuum left by the Minoans' decline paved the way for the rise of the Mycenaeans, who assimilated elements of Minoan culture into their society.

The Mycenaeans, hailing from mainland Greece, established their dominance over Crete during the Late Bronze Age (circa 1600-1100 BCE). Their fortified citadels, such as Mycenae and Tiryns, bear witness to their military prowess and organizational sophistication. The Mycenaeans adopted aspects of Minoan culture, including writing systems, artistic styles, and religious practices, further enriching the cultural mosaic of Crete.

Crete's strategic significance continued into classical antiquity as the island became an integral part of Greek history and mythology. According to legend, Crete was the birthplace of Zeus, the king of the Olympian gods, and the site of the labyrinth constructed by Daedalus to contain the Minotaur.

Throughout subsequent centuries, Crete experienced various conquerors and cultures, including Roman, Byzantine, Venetian, and Ottoman influences. Each successive civilization left its imprint on the island's landscape, architecture, and traditions, contributing to Crete's cultural heritage.

REFERENCES
- Castleden, Rodney. "Minoans: Life in Bronze Age Crete." Routledge, 2002.
- Branigan, Keith. "The Foundations of Palatial Crete: A Survey of Crete in the Early Bronze Age." Routledge, 2013.
- Davaras, Costis. "Crete: Culture and Civilization." Ekdotike Athenon, 2004.

Solar Analemma Defined

The solar analemma, a celestial phenomenon, manifests as a figure-eight-shaped curve when the position of the Sun in the sky is plotted at the same time each day over the course of a year. Its formation is intricately tied to the Earth's axial tilt and its elliptical orbit around the Sun. This phenomenon offers valuable insights into the dynamics of Earth's motion in space.

The axial tilt of the Earth, approximately 23.5 degrees relative to its orbital plane, causes the Sun's apparent north-south deviations throughout the year. These deviations lead to the characteristic loops of the analemma, with the northern loop representing the Sun's highest point during the summer solstice and the southern loop corresponding to its lowest point during the winter solstice. These loops demonstrate the Sun's declination, its angular distance north or south of the celestial equator.

Additionally, the Earth's elliptical orbit introduces an east-west shift in the analemma, reflecting the variation in the length of days throughout the year. This shift occurs due to the non-uniform motion of the Earth along its orbit, with the Sun sometimes appearing slightly ahead or behind its mean position.

REFERENCE:

- "Astronomy Picture of the Day" by NASA (https://apod.nasa.gov/apod/ap170520.html) and academic articles like "The Solar Analemma" by Meeus (https://www.springer.com/gp/book/9789401090060)

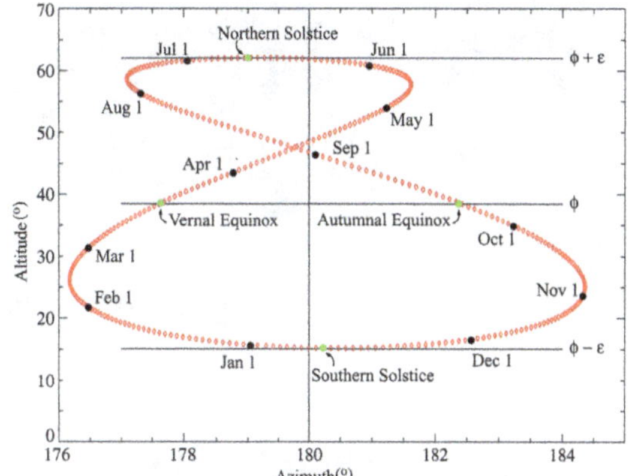

Photo of Analemma Sun path By PAR - JPL Horizons, Public Domain, https://commons.wikimedia.org/w/index.php?curid=3111462

Phaistos Disc Defined

The Phaistos Disc is a unique archaeological artifact discovered in 1908 by Italian archaeologist Luigi Pernier at the Minoan palace site of Phaistos on the island of Crete. Dating back to the Minoan Bronze Age, approximately 1700 BCE, the disc is made of fired clay and features a spiral of stamped symbols on both sides.

Despite numerous attempts to decipher its meaning, the symbols on the Phaistos Disc remain undeciphered, and its purpose remains uncertain. The disc is inscribed with 241 individual symbols, comprising 45 unique signs, arranged in a clockwise spiral pattern from the disc's periphery to its center. The symbols depict various objects, animals, and human figures, leading to speculation that they may represent a form of writing, religious symbols, or even a decorative pattern.

Scholars have proposed various theories regarding the origin, purpose, and meaning of the disc, ranging from a religious or ceremonial artifact to a form of writing or accounting system. However, due to the lack of similar artifacts or decipherable linguistic context, the true significance of the Phaistos Disc remains elusive.

REFERENCES:

- "The Phaistos Disk" by Harriet Blitzer, American Journal of Archaeology, Vol. 96, No. 3 (July 1992), pp. 543-544.
- "The Phaistos Disk: A New Way of Approaching a Famous Enigma" by Gareth Owens, Journal of Mediterranean Archaeology, Vol. 20, No. 1 (2007), pp. 135-139.

Photos of Side A and Side B of the Phaistos Disc from public domain detailing both sides.

Artifact Characteristics

Artifact characteristics observed provide possible proof that the disc was not used directly by an observer and was only intended to be a template.

The artifact did not provide a proper observable character visualization for the viewer and was not meant to be used directly as a perceptible device. The size of the artifact, in relation to the complexity of the layout and the symbols on it, makes the device challenging to understand. The closeup view of symbols clarifies this stance.

Picture at left shows a close-up view of the shoulder yoke with tiny details of vase tops within the yoke bar. Picture at right shows very slight detail, almost unseen by the naked eye, of plant growth scallops along the left edge of the crop seed planting symbol. These images were taken from the author's public domain image.

Other characteristics of the disc that detract direct observation include the depth of stamping less obvious symbol differences (several stamps to create the disc were used, showing the slightly deviated constructs were intentional), all in reverse contrast to the majority of the clay surface area.

This construction technique, however, is perfect in its ability to reveal those details when used as a suitable template to make clay press stamps. The details that are most hidden and unobservable by the causal observation of the disc come out in stunning detail when printed upon parchments, hidden clay tablets, or even wall tiles. Though the author's attempt at printing from the clay stamps created from the disc is poor compared to the actual disc-defined symbology, it immediately displayed a still stunning definition of the symbols and was repeated on multiple printed papers.

The final definitive information resides in the printed copy from the clay stamps. This is witnessed in the ink-printed design by the author, as it clearly displays the entirety of the symbol designs located on both sides of the Phaistos Disc, making it easy to observe the intended structure of the symbol groups and divisions. It is impossible to observe the entire layout from both sides of the artifact.

Phaistos Disc as a Bi-Faced Template for Reproducing Clay Mold Stamps

An air-dry clay was used by the author, which was rolled out and then pressed into the side of the replica artifact to make reversed images of the stamped symbols and spirals on each side. Then, the two clay stamps were cut circularly and glued together in the proper direction to one another. The appropriate 'hinge' point for alignment is the five dotted lines on each side of the artifact face, which denotes where the observer would read before moving to the center of the opposite side to continue the yearly calendar viewing.

The gauge depths of the individual stamps change and cause a notable height difference in the final clay stamp areas that would contact the surfaces, thus making stamp sets from the disc seem problematic. However, the very defined and deep grooving of the symbols never gets full clay imprinting to the full depth but instead creates an air barrier in those deep channels when pressing, which eases the release of the blanks being stamped.

This process is further enhanced by controlling the thickness of the clay blank to a thinner layer, which can be backed by a thick sponge or other suitable membrane that gives for a pressure pad. This allows the pressure to conform more equally around the disc, allowing the thinner clay blank to warp into the deeper symbol image reliefs more, providing a more uniform raised height of the finished symbols.

The author used a 1-inch scrubbing pad of medium stiffness to apply pressure over each region, only pressing on about three-square inches at a time around the entire surface. This variable pressure quickly created a very uniform surface paper that could conform to that allowed the proper inking of every symbol. Initial attempts at a thicker bed of clay for the stamp blank proved unable to conform, so the thin section pressing blank proved vital.

After the stamp blanks were pressed and released from the disc replica, they were laid onto a glass piece to flatten out the various raised dimpled areas where deeper disc symbols were present. This allowed the author to tap the glass down onto the table, which flattened the stamped surfaces. Once trimmed round and dried, the two halves were popped off the glass and glued back to back in proper clocked positions to attempt stamping paper.

The clay stamps were used to make up to three page stampings before needing to be covered again with ink using a simple ink transfer rubber hand roller. As an air-dry clay, the stamps were weaker than fired clay, but a total of twelve pages were pressed with no visible wear to the stamp sets.

It became evident that authentic parchment would provide a more suitable floppy surface to press to instead of modern paper. Even easier would be to use hide surfaces, as hide conforms to the deviated heights of the symbols. Clay tiles would provide the best transfer medium as height would not matter for symbols and could likely avoid the inking process altogether, as it could then be touch painted in the reliefs.

One attempt was made to double ink two colors for symbol recognition before stamping, but the author was unable to perform such complex inking without tactics that were fast enough to avoid the ink drying between sets. Using transfer ink that is oil-based provided the best outcome, as it dried in hours instead of minutes, giving time for the ink to press slower, causing a sticky tactile feel that allowed for the partial removal and relaying of paper to check if stamping was complete. With this ink, wrapping the paper onto both sides at once gave a solid hinged area that never gave a double-printed symbol issue when reapplying the paper to the surface to better ink regions missed.

Photo by author: clay imprints taken from the artifact to use as ink stamps after use. The left single stamp is a 3D-printed image of this that worked very well, too.

Printing Layout

To make the print using paper or hide, one would wrap the paper or hide around the two inked sides of the stamps, aligning the folded hinge of the paper or hide in line with the aligned five dot segments so they would oppose each other and remain inline on the final printed piece. After pressing, the paper or hide is peeled away, one side at a time, to reveal the finished analemma. One could single-side stamp various objects like bricks, tiles, wood, walls, clothes, and pelts as well.

The inked surface is meant to be viewed with each circular hemisphere beside each other horizontally, with the Side A hemisphere to the left as the 'start' of the year.

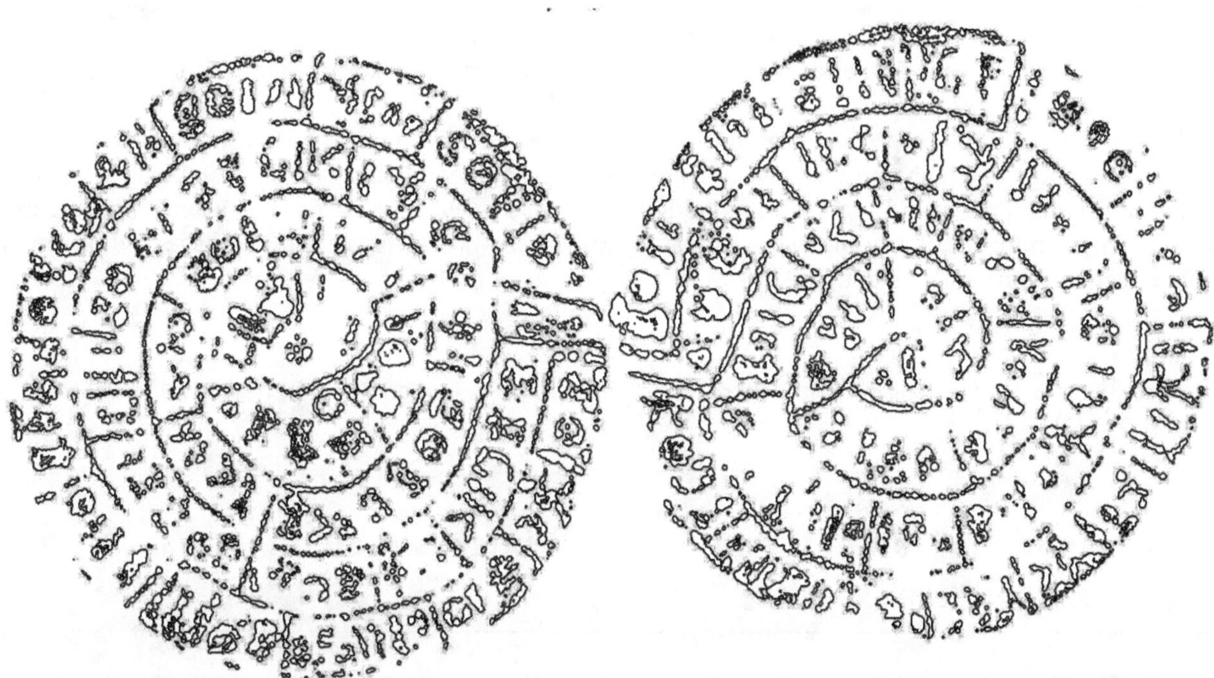

Scan by author: a reproduced print on paper after proper wrapping around the inked dual-faced opposing stamps. A crisp edge connection exists centrally connecting the multiple dotted line areas on both sides. The analemma of the solar precession through the sky is represented in the Ancient Universal Language using the Sun's shadow marks instead of the apparent Sun's location in the sky. This is because it is impossible to directly reference the Sun's slight movements daily in the open sky, whereas it is easy to do so on a shadow line. This reverses the apparent circular (represented by spirals indicating apparent Sun movement in each hemisphere of the analemma) motion of the actual Sun direction. It appears the creator of the artifact maintained a balanced look on each side of the disc by keeping the apparent spiral directions the same in a counterclockwise direction when stamped. Usually, apparent analemma spirals would reverse in the path shown in Figure 8.

Printing Press Background

The evidence of the first ancient printing press comes from archaeological discoveries and historical records dating back to ancient China. The earliest known printing press dates to the Tang Dynasty (618-907 AD), where woodblock printing techniques were utilized. This printing method involved carving characters or images into wooden blocks, which were then inked and pressed onto paper to produce multiple copies of texts or illustrations.

Archaeological findings, such as surviving wooden printing blocks and printed materials, provide tangible evidence of early printing practices in ancient China. These artifacts offer insights into the technological advancements and cultural significance of printing during this period. Additionally, historical texts and records from the Tang Dynasty mention the use of woodblock printing for producing Buddhist scriptures, official documents, and literary works, further confirming the existence and widespread adoption of printing presses in ancient China.

The development of woodblock printing in ancient China laid the foundation for later advancements in printing technology, including movable type printing during the Song Dynasty (960-1279 AD) and the introduction of printing presses in Europe during the Renaissance. The evidence of the first ancient printing press highlights the importance of printing in disseminating knowledge, preserving cultural heritage, and facilitating communication in ancient civilizations.

REFERENCE:
- Title: "The Origins of Printing in China" Author: Tsien Tsuen-Hsuin Publication: The British Library, 1985 ISBN: 978-0712301356

The Ancient Division of Summer and Winter in Calendars Similar to the Phaistos Disc

The ancient calendar divisions of only summer and winter were prevalent in various ancient societies, particularly those with temperate climates where the seasonal changes were more pronounced. While specific details varied among different cultures, the general division into two main seasons, summer and winter, was common in many ancient calendars.

Ancient Cultures:

- **Mesopotamia:** The ancient Mesopotamians, including the Sumerians, Babylonians, and Assyrians, recognized two main seasons: summer and winter. These divisions were based on observations of temperature changes, rainfall patterns, and agricultural activities. Summer was associated with hot, dry weather and the growing season, while winter brought cooler temperatures and a dormant period for agriculture.

- **Egypt:** In ancient Egypt, the calendar was closely tied to the annual flooding of the Nile River, which marked the beginning of the agricultural year. The flooding, which typically occurred during the summer months, facilitated the cultivation of crops and was associated with the season of abundance and growth. Winter, on the other hand, was a time of lower temperatures and reduced agricultural activity as the Nile receded and the land lay fallow.

- **Greece:** Ancient Greek calendars varied by region and city-state, but many followed a similar pattern based on agricultural cycles. The Greeks recognized two main seasons, summer and winter, which corresponded roughly to the warm and cold periods of the year. Summer was associated with longer days, warmer temperatures, and the cultivation of crops, while winter brought shorter days, cooler temperatures, and the need to prepare for the colder months ahead.

- **Rome:** The ancient Roman calendar, influenced by Etruscan and Greek traditions, also recognized two main seasons: summer and winter. Summer was a time of agricultural activity, festivals, and outdoor events, while winter brought colder temperatures, shorter days, and the need to prepare for the hardships of the colder months. The Roman festivals of Saturnalia and Floralia, for example, celebrated the transition from winter to spring and the renewal of life in nature.

In summary, the division of the ancient calendars into only summer and winter was standard in many ancient societies, particularly those with temperate climates where the seasonal changes were prominent. These divisions were based on observations of temperature variations, agricultural cycles, and natural phenomena, and they played a crucial role in organizing daily life, religious festivals, and farming activities in ancient times.

REFERENCES
- Van de Mieroop, Marc. "A History of the Ancient Near East, ca. 3000-323 BC." Blackwell Publishing, 2007.
- Cartledge, Paul. "The Greeks: A Portrait of Self and Others." Oxford University Press, 2002.
- Beard, Mary, et al. "The Oxford Classical Dictionary." Oxford University Press, 2012.

Season Dates are Defined in Two Ways: Astronomical Definition and Meteorological Definition.

Meteorological definition used within the Phaistos Disc:

- **Spring:** March 1st to May 31st in the Northern Hemisphere (NH) and September 1st to November 30th in the Southern Hemisphere (SH).

- **Summer:** June 1st to August 31st in the Northern Hemisphere (NH) and December 1st to February 28th/29th in the Southern Hemisphere (SH).

- **Autumn (Fall):** September 1st to November 30th in the Northern Hemisphere (NH) and March 1st to May 31st in the Southern Hemisphere (SH).

- **Winter:** December 1st to February 28th/29th in the Northern Hemisphere (NH) and June 1st to August 31st in the Southern Hemisphere (SH).

These dates are based on the calendar months and represent the divisions of the year commonly used by meteorologists to simplify climate data analysis and forecasting. Unlike the astronomical definition, which is based on astronomical events such as solstices and equinoxes, the meteorological definition divides the year into four seasons of approximately equal length based on temperature patterns and climate conditions observed over time.

Background

The ancient usage of seasons, particularly in agricultural societies, often revolved around the beginning of the months rather than specific astronomical events like solstices and equinoxes. In many ancient civilizations, including those of Mesopotamia, Egypt, Greece, and Rome, the calendar was closely tied to agricultural cycles, with each month representing a distinct phase of the farming year. This system allowed communities to coordinate planting, harvesting, and other agricultural activities based on the seasonal changes observed in their local environment.

- **Mesopotamia:** In ancient Mesopotamia, one of the earliest known civilizations, the calendar was lunar-based, with each month beginning with the sighting of the new moon. The Babylonians, for example, had a calendar consisting of twelve lunar months, each beginning with the appearance of the new crescent moon. The agricultural calendar of Mesopotamia was divided into two main seasons: the "summer" season, corresponding roughly to the months from April to September, and the "winter" season, from

October to March. These seasons were based on observations of temperature changes, rainfall patterns, and agricultural activities such as planting and harvesting.

- **Egypt:** Ancient Egypt also had a calendar based on agricultural cycles, particularly the flooding of the Nile River, which was crucial for agriculture in the region. The Egyptian calendar consisted of twelve months, each beginning with the heliacal rising of the star Sirius, which coincided with the annual flooding of the Nile. The flooding of the Nile marked the start of the agricultural year and the onset of the planting season. The Egyptian calendar also divided the year into three seasons: Akhet (Inundation), Peret (Growth), and Shemu (Harvest).

- **Greece:** In ancient Greece, the calendar varied by region and city-state, but it generally followed a similar pattern based on agricultural activities. The Athenian calendar, for example, was divided into twelve lunar months, with each month beginning with the sighting of the new moon. The months were named after various agricultural events or religious festivals, reflecting the seasonal rhythms of farming life. The Greeks also recognized the importance of seasonal changes, with festivals and rituals dedicated to agricultural deities such as Demeter and Dionysus.

- **Rome:** The Roman calendar, influenced by Etruscan and Greek traditions, was divided into twelve months, beginning with March (Martius). The Roman agricultural calendar was closely tied to religious festivals and observances, with each month marked by rituals honoring the gods and goddesses associated with farming, fertility, and the changing seasons. The Roman festivals of Saturnalia and Floralia, for example, celebrated the sowing and flowering of crops in the spring.

In conclusion, the ancient usage of seasons starting at the beginning of the months instead of solstices and equinoxes reflects the close relationship between the calendar, agricultural cycles, and religious observances in ancient civilizations. By organizing time according to the phases of the moon and the seasonal changes observed in their environment, ancient societies were able to coordinate their agricultural activities and mark the passage of time with rituals and festivals that celebrated the cycles of nature.

Both Versions of Seasonal Start Dates

- Astronomical Definition:

  - **Definition:** The astronomical definition of seasons is based on the position of the Earth in relation to the Sun. It divides the year into four seasons: spring, summer, autumn (fall), and winter. These seasons are determined by the Earth's tilt on its axis and its orbit around the Sun.

  - **Key Marker:** Astronomical seasons are marked by specific astronomical events, including the spring equinox, summer solstice, autumn equinox, and winter solstice. These events occur when the tilt of the Earth's axis is either towards or away from the Sun, resulting in changes in the length of daylight and temperature.

  - **Consistency:** Astronomical seasons are consistent globally, meaning that they occur at the same time for everyone, regardless of location. For example, the summer solstice in the Northern Hemisphere always falls around June 21st.

- Meteorological Definition:

  - **Definition:** The meteorological definition of seasons is based on temperature patterns and climate conditions. It divides the year into four seasons of approximately three months each: spring (March-May), summer (June-August), autumn (September-November), and winter (December-February).

  - **Key Marker:** Meteorological seasons are based on the annual temperature cycle and weather patterns rather than astronomical events. They are typically defined by the calendar months, with each season representing the average weather conditions observed during that period.

- **Variability:** Meteorological seasons may vary depending on geographic location and local climate conditions. For example, regions near the equator may not experience distinct seasons based on temperature variations, while polar regions may have longer or shorter seasons.

In summary, the astronomical definition of seasons is based on the Earth's position relative to the Sun. Seasons are marked by specific astronomical events, whereas the meteorological definition of season is based on temperature patterns and climate conditions observed over time. While astronomical seasons are consistent globally, meteorological seasons may vary depending on geographic location and local climate.

REFERENCES:

- Parpola, Simo. "The Helsinki Atlas of the Near East in the Neo-Assyrian Period." Helsinki University Press, 2001.
- Parker, Robert. "Miasma: Pollution and Purification in Early Greek Religion." Oxford University Press, 1996.
- Scarre, Chris, et al. "The Human Past: World Prehistory and the Development of Human Societies." Thames & Hudson, 2018.

The Athenian Calendar: A Unique Division of Months

In ancient Greece, the Athenians employed a distinctive calendar system that divided their year into two phases, reflecting the agricultural and religious rhythms of their society. This calendar, known as the Attic calendar, consisted of twelve lunar months organized into two distinct periods: the Dry Season and the Rainy Season. The Athenian calendar provides valuable insights into the ancient Greeks' understanding of time, the natural world, and their religious practices.

The Athenian Calendar:

The Athenian calendar was based on the lunar cycle, with each month corresponding roughly to the phases of the Moon. However, unlike other Greek city-states that utilized a single twelve-month calendar, *the Athenians divided their year into two distinct phases, each comprising six months. These phases were determined by the agricultural and climatic conditions prevalent in Attica, the region surrounding Athens.*

- **The Dry Season (May to October):** The first phase of the Athenian calendar, known as the dry season, encompassed the months from May to October. This period coincided with the warmer, drier months of the year when agricultural activities such as planting, harvesting, and winemaking were prevalent. The months of the dry season were characterized by festivals celebrating fertility, agriculture, and the harvest, including the Thargelia, Apollo, and Artemis, and the Eleusinian Mysteries, honoring Demeter and Persephone.

- **The Rainy Season (November to April):** The second phase of the Athenian calendar, known as the rainy season, spanned the months from November to April. This period coincided with the cooler, wetter months of the year when rainfall was abundant and agricultural activities were less prevalent. The months of the rainy season were associated with religious festivals, purification rites, and rituals aimed at appeasing the gods and ensuring the fertility of the land. Among these festivals were the Panathenaea, honoring Athena, and the Anthesteria, celebrating Dionysus.

Divisions of Month

The Athenian calendar, *while primarily divided into two seasons, also had a unique daily division within each month. The days within Athenian months were organized into cycles known as "dekads," with each dekad consisting of ten days.* This system of dekads provided a more granular division of time within the Athenian month, allowing for precise tracking of daily activities, religious observances, and civic duties.

- **Structure of Athenian Months:** *Each Athenian month was comprised of three dekads, totaling thirty days. These thirty-day months were based on the lunar cycle, with each dekad corresponding roughly to one-third of the lunar month.* The first dekad of the month was known as the "proton," the second dekad as the "deuteran," and the third dekad as the "tritan."

- **Athenian Calendar Example:** For example, let's consider the Athenian month of Hekatombaion, which roughly corresponds to July/August in the modern calendar. In the Athenian calendar, Hekatombaion consisted of three dekads, each containing ten days.

  - Proton: Days 1-10

  - Deuteran: Days 11-20

  - Tritan: Days 21-30

  Within each dekad, the days were numbered sequentially from one to ten. For instance, in the Proton dekad of Hekatombaion, the days would be numbered 1-10, representing the first ten days of the month. Similarly, the Deuteran dekad would encompass days 11-20, and the Tritan dekad would include days 21-30.

- **Cultural and Religious Significance:** The division of Athenian months into dekads held cultural, religious, and practical significance in ancient Greek society. Each dekad was associated with particular religious festivals, civic events, and agricultural activities. The careful organization of time into dekads allowed Athenian citizens to plan their daily lives, observe religious rites, and participate in communal celebrations with precision and regularity.

- **Other Divided Month Calendars in Ancient Greece:** While the Athenian calendar is perhaps the most well-known example of a divided-month calendar in ancient Greece, other Greek city-states may have employed similar systems. *The city-state of Corinth, for example, is believed to have used a calendar divided into two six-month periods, reflecting the region's agricultural and climatic conditions.*

REFERENCES:
- Parker, Robert. "Miasma: Pollution and Purification in Early Greek Religion." Oxford University Press, 1996.
- Rutherford, Ian. "Athenian Religion: A History." Oxford University Press, 2000.
- Wycherley, R. E. "The Athenian Calendar." Harvard Studies in Classical Philology, Vol. 74 (1970), pp. 159-183.
- Young, Rodney S. "The Athenian Festivals: A Commentary." Oxford University Press, 2010.

The First Iteration Calendar

The first iteration of the Roman calendar, traditionally attributed to Romulus, the legendary founder of Rome, consisted of ten months and marked the early stages of Roman society's attempts to organize time. This primitive calendar, known as the Romulan calendar, served as the foundation for later developments in the Roman calendar system. While there is limited historical documentation on the specifics of this early calendar, various ancient sources and modern scholarship provide insights into its structure, organization, and ties to both Roman and Greek societies.

- **Origins and Structure:** The Romulan calendar, according to Roman tradition, began with the founding of Rome in 753 BCE. *It consisted of ten months, totaling 304 days, and reflected the agricultural and seasonal rhythms prevalent in ancient Italy. The ten months were named Martius (March), Aprilis (April), Maius (May), Junius (June), Quintilis (July), Sextilis (August), September, October, November, and December.*

- **Greek Influence:** The Romulan calendar likely bore some influence from the Greek lunar calendar, which also consisted of ten months. This influence is not surprising given the cultural and commercial exchanges between early Rome and the Greek colonies in southern Italy. However, while the Greek calendar was based on lunar cycles, the Romulan calendar was primarily a solar calendar, with each month roughly corresponding to the cycles of the Moon.

- **Exclusion of Winter Months:** *One notable characteristic of the Romulan calendar was the exclusion of the winter months, namely January and February. This omission reflects the agricultural focus of the early Roman calendar, which prioritized the growing season and ignored the less agriculturally significant winter months. The absence of these months created a gap in the calendar, leading to an imbalance in the reckoning of time and necessitating later reforms.*

- **Festivals and Religious Observances:** The Romulan calendar was closely intertwined with religious festivals and observances, reflecting the religious beliefs and practices of early Roman society. Each month was marked by various religious rites and ceremonies dedicated to the gods and goddesses of the Roman pantheon. For example, Martius was named after Mars, the god of war, and featured festivals honoring Mars and other deities associated with warfare and agriculture.

- **Transition to the Julian Calendar:** Despite its early prominence, the Romulan calendar underwent significant reforms over time, particularly during the Republican and Imperial periods of Roman history. The most notable reform occurred during the reign of Julius Caesar in 46 BCE when the Julian calendar was introduced. This calendar, based on the solar year and incorporating leap years, replaced the old Romulan calendar, establishing the foundation for the modern Gregorian calendar used today.

REFERENCES:

- Beard, M., North, J., & Price, S. (1998). "Religions of Rome: Volume 1, A History." Cambridge University Press.
- Forsythe, G. (2005). "A Critical History of Early Rome: From Prehistory to the First Punic War." University of California Press.
- Ogilvie, R. M. (1986). "The Romans and Their Gods in the Age of Augustus." Routledge.

Phaistos Disc Segments in Relation to The Solar Analemma

The crafting of the artifact took incredible thought as the harmonious flow and segmenting to match specific significant correlations to the solar analemma are present in an absolutely brilliant way.

Side A of the artifact is a product of perfection. The spring flower symbol is central, and the March 1st month group resides as the last group of Side B. This frees up room by default, but as the analemma clocking dictates, the month date begins first before the spring sunrise, bringing in the New Year. To avoid confusion, the author presents January 1st as the new year in this report. However, it is evident that this disc begins the year on Side A in the center, making it the New Year and the first day of the summer side (though it is clear the designer displays all four seasons that start at the beginning day of the month's solstices and equinoxes fall on throughout the year).

Immediately after the March 15 month group, the March 21 spring equinox symbol group is listed. The four important points the author highlighted, the lily and flower symbols in yellow, appear to be mostly aligned with one another as observed from the center to the outside.

An undeniable addition to a symbol resides in the March 15 monthly group with the long "plant" symbol. As you observe the lower tail of it, the designer carved a continuing line outward into the next spiral, "crossing over" the two. This is important, as this continued line, in fact, crosses the symbols for the first solar crossover event of the analemma. This could be a telling of what the long plant symbol stands for. Note that in the June 1 month group, there is again a plant symbol that aligns with that crossover symbol.

Author-modified image from public domain: side A has been modified by author 2024 to reveal essential dates in relation to the disc's design element. Visually, it is appealing in the harmonious way important dates are shown in a balanced format with regard to the solar analemma. Note the way the months May 1, May 15, and June 15 appear perfectly separated from one another, which may indicate reasoning for similar symbol groups.

Next, you observe leaving the inner spirals at the 'crossover' line of the summer solstice. This again completes a perfect division of the side.

Immediately following the symbol group's order, the unique flower symbol emerges on the July 1 season group, which signifies it is considered the 'first month' or 'second new year' after the solstice. This parallels the divisions almost identically on Side B of the winter solstice group and the January 1 group 'New Year.' The author believes this is the first-ever double new year, or 'divided year' that indicates two new-year events, as nothing can be found in researching that suggests such an event in history.

Again, the term 'new year' for these combinations for both first-month listings immediately following, is named by the author; but could mean 'divisions' or 'halfway', as the true and beginning 'New Year' is listed as March 1st to start the calendar.

As noted, the March 1 flower, followed by the flower symbol on the March 21 equinox, is centrally located between the equinoxes (and their flower symbols) in a similar format of separation. However, the month of March 15th falls between those symbols, so instead of the approximate seven-day spread, these two dates (flowers) spread around twenty-one days. This arrangement of the three equilateral divisions of the flower symbol in comparison to the analemma events is undeniable. Add the September 24 lily symbol equally distanced (to the other lilies on solstices), and the observable divided arrangement use is solid.

On another note, the real analemma has about a fifteen-day offset from the bottom alignment of the solstice to the top alignment to solstice. The author states that this rendition on the disc is the best way to take out that sideways shift in nature and return it to a perfectly aligned calendar rendering.

The last noted event is the September 1 month group, which is final and displayed on Side A due to the fact is falls three days before the solar crossover event.

Image from public domain modified by author 2024: important Side B dates.

Side B shows a similar remarkable balance to Side A. The second solar crossover event of the analemma season may be represented in the 90-degree angled line around the first group. The crossover happens on August 3rd, which is why the August 1 month group is presented as the last group on Side A. This also helps maintain the smaller starting symbol of the helmet and division wavy line group, as drawing space is limited.

The 90-degree line that connects through the equinox group is possibly relevant.

The winter solstice group resides alone, and then the New Year 'crossover' before the January 1st group provides the ending to the central spiral.

February 1 holiday is listed before the edge spiral completes with the March 1st monthly group, where again the user would cross the dots over to the center of Side A for the start of the summer side (and spring season.)

Phaistos Disc Symbol Definitions and Placement

Please note many of the symbols present will not be directly discussed in singular meaning or purpose as they do not present as much importance to the discussion on the purpose of describing the artifact in this paper, mainly due to such things as randomness, low repeat count, or unknown structural meaning to the described outline of the calendar, which they expressly focus on in this document. However, some will be described within groupings of each other. Note several symbol images are missing important variations described later.

Symbols

Image from public domain: possible symbol meanings, though the author disagrees with some as described later. https://en.wikipedia.org/wiki/Phaistos_Disc

Symbol Grouping Appearance:

It would appear that the majority of the symbols groups reside within the central spiral section of the disc sides, but that is misleading as there are eighteen sections within and twelve sections, plus the lily group, along the outside single row. This difference of only five groups more along the inside spiral is due to the volume of space along the outer rim compared to the cramped spacing inside.

There are 61 groups of symbols, 31 on Side A and 30 on Side B, possibly comprising 242 occurrences from at least 45 distinct symbols. Still, it is believed each minuscule change in a stamp of a symbol is a different symbol related to the recognized symbol it most closely mimics. The numbers 01-45 shown were made by Arthur Evans, so used here with a few changed expressions of the symbols, which will be referenced in their respective group numbers listed below.

The labels A1-A31 and B1-B30 are the traditional word numbers.[14]

Side A:

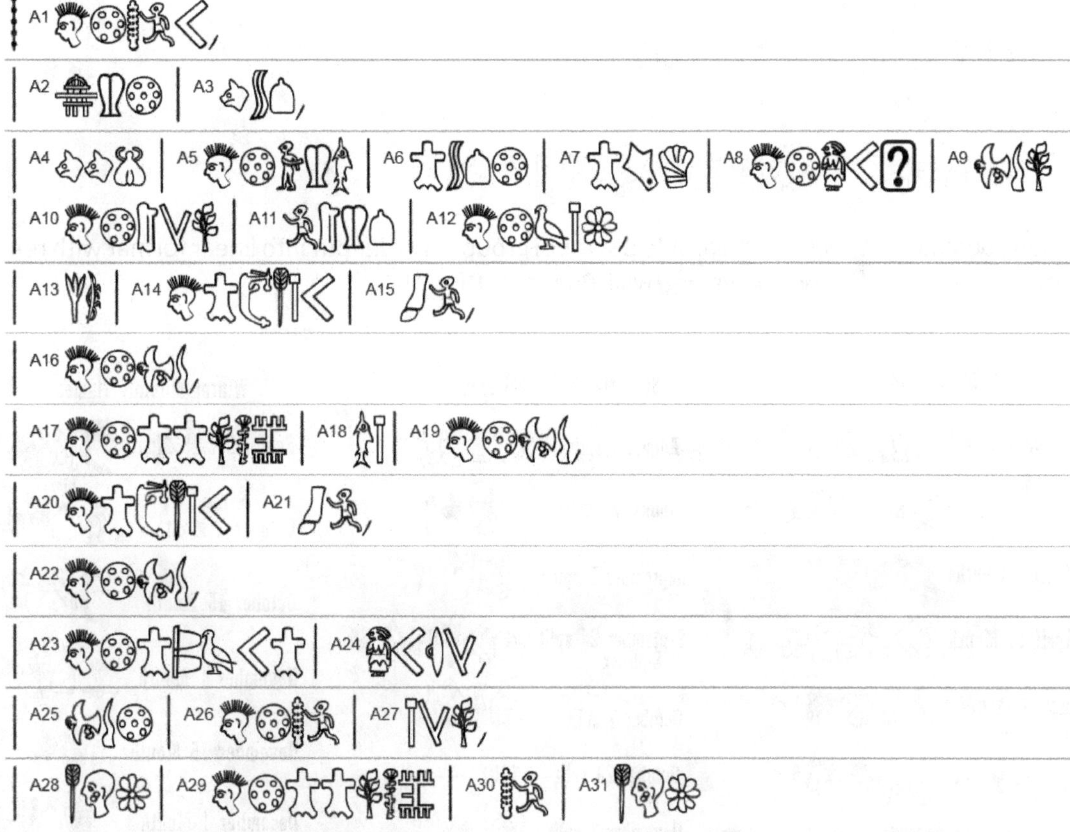

Image sourced from public domain: Side A symbol groups in order put into linear format with referenced designators. https://en.wikipedia.org/wiki/Phaistos_Disc

Side B:

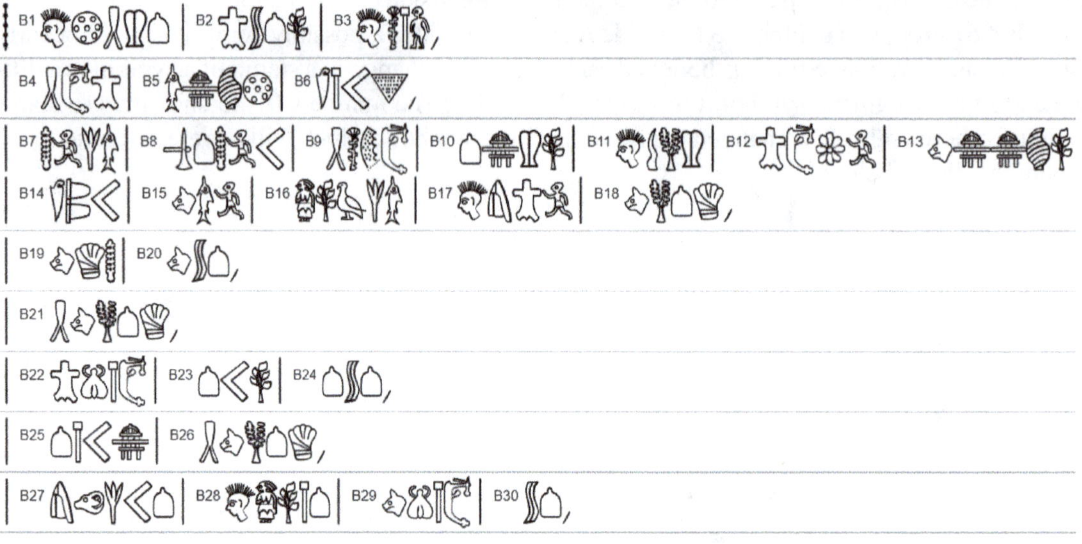

Image sourced from public domain: Side B symbol groups in order put into linear format with referenced designators. https://en.wikipedia.org/wiki/Phaistos_Disc

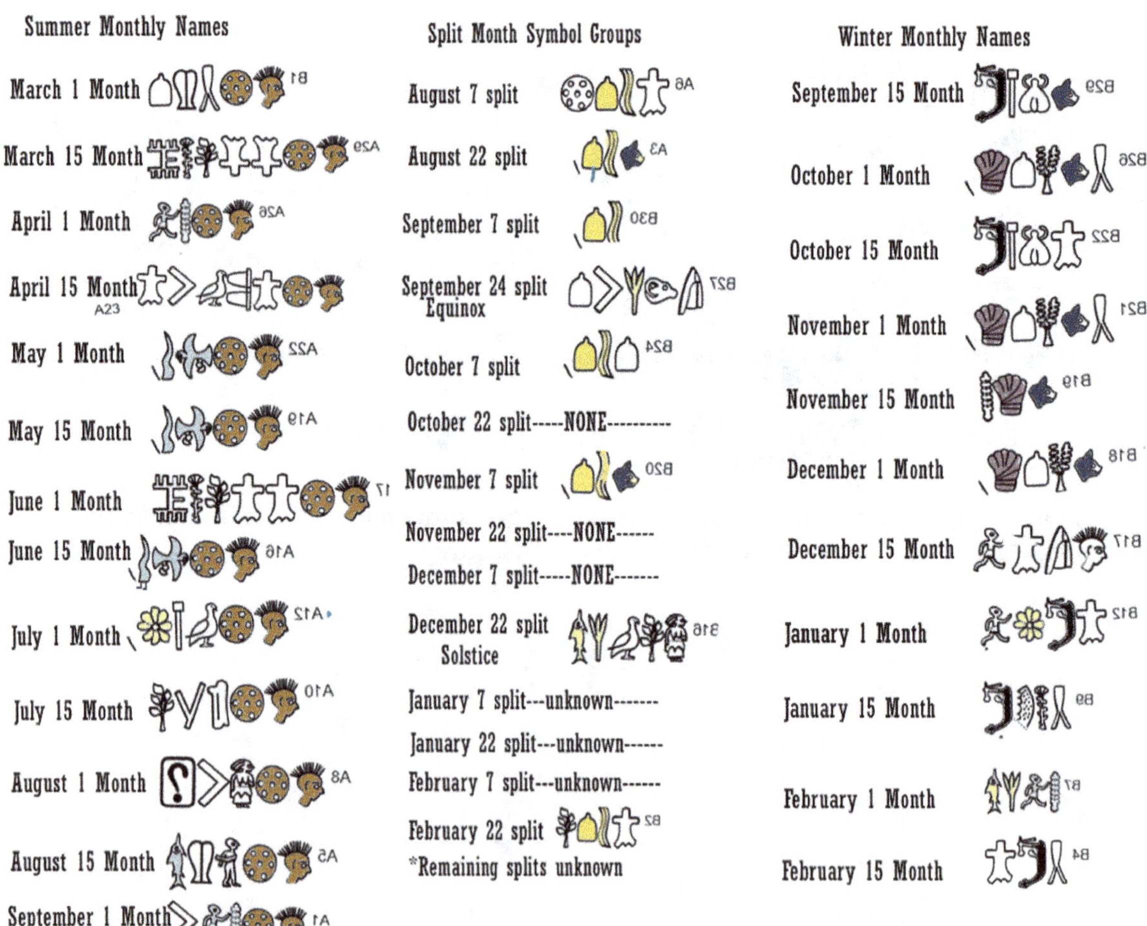

Author's rendition of monthly and split-month symbol groups. A complete representation of possible split months is not possible without much speculation. Other splits may be incorporated into groupings that designate more critical information. The split month groups represented possibly represent the meaning of the ribbon symbol, as determined by the author in most instances. Possible events that interfere with such ongoing display use include proximity groups for equinox, solstice and new years. More discussion on the wavy line symbol exists on the topic later on in the report.

Symbol Group Placement Along Calendar Solar Analemma

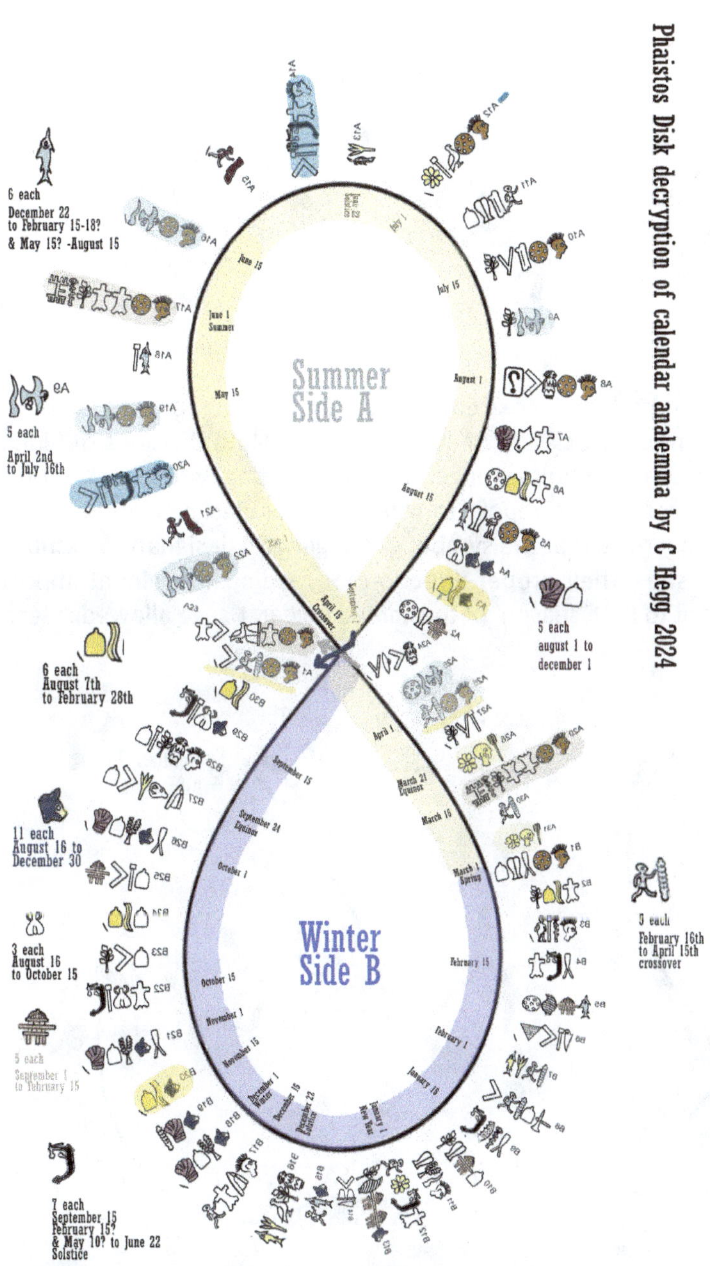

Copyright image design rendered and created by the author of symbol groups on the Phaistos Disc calendar in association with the solar analemma 2024. Usage of rendering allowed with reference to this report name.

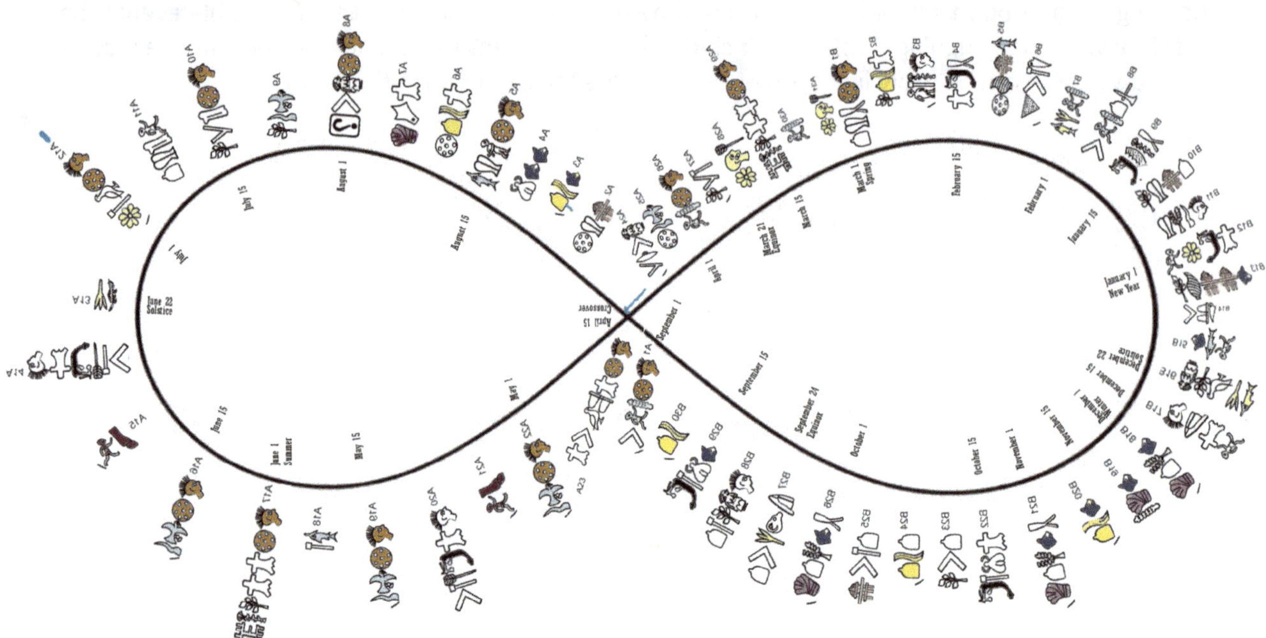

Copyright image rendered and created by author showing proper stamped direction reading horizontally of analemma association of symbol groups. Note divisions of Side A in yellow and Side B in blue of the artifact as symbols arranged in order starting with March 1st month top center right lobe. See detailed listings in the report to reference detailed descriptions of essential placements and symbol decryption. Note that the symbol group general designation number is backward as each group is reversed to show their proper direction for reading. Prominent important symbols around the image are relevant to that 'season' of the calendar year. Usage allowed referencing of this report's name and author.

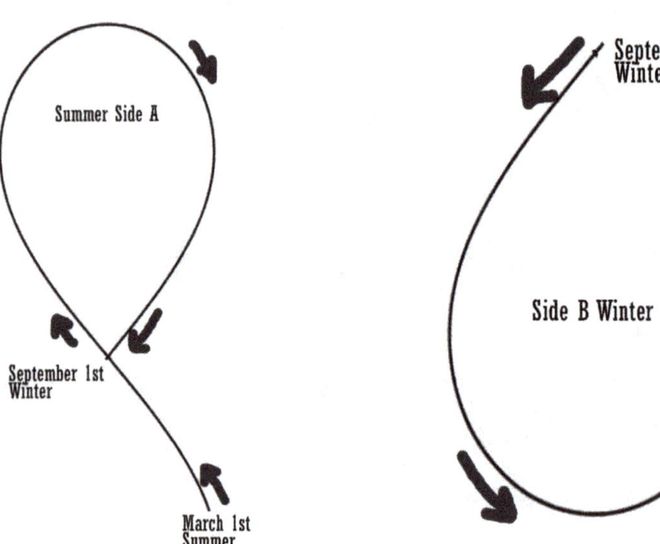

Images showing sides of disc beginning and ending as it relates to the generalized solar analemma figure 8 and directions of travel of the sun shadow.

Symbol Group Coverage of Analemma Sections

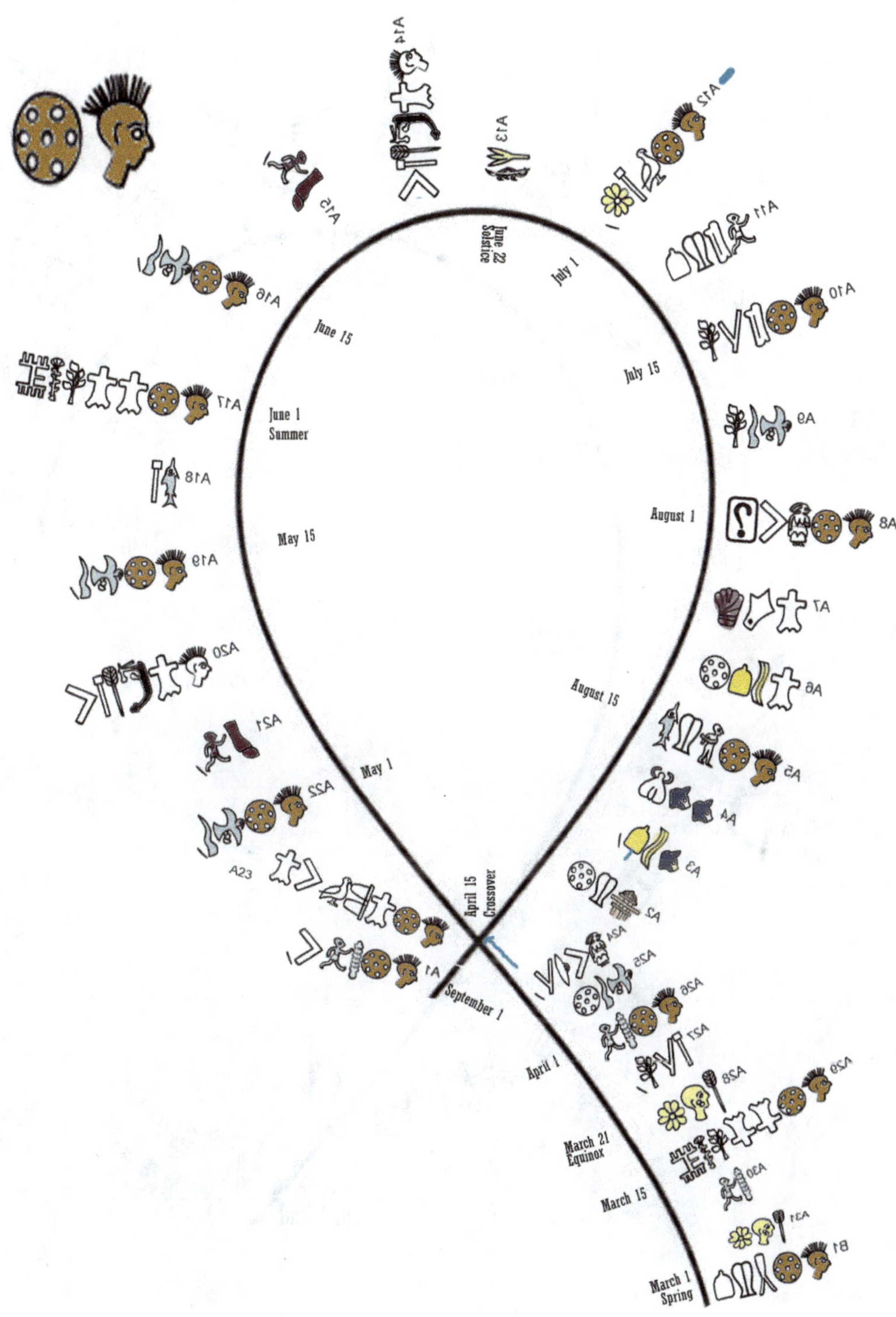

Wheel and Plumed Head Group Coverage.

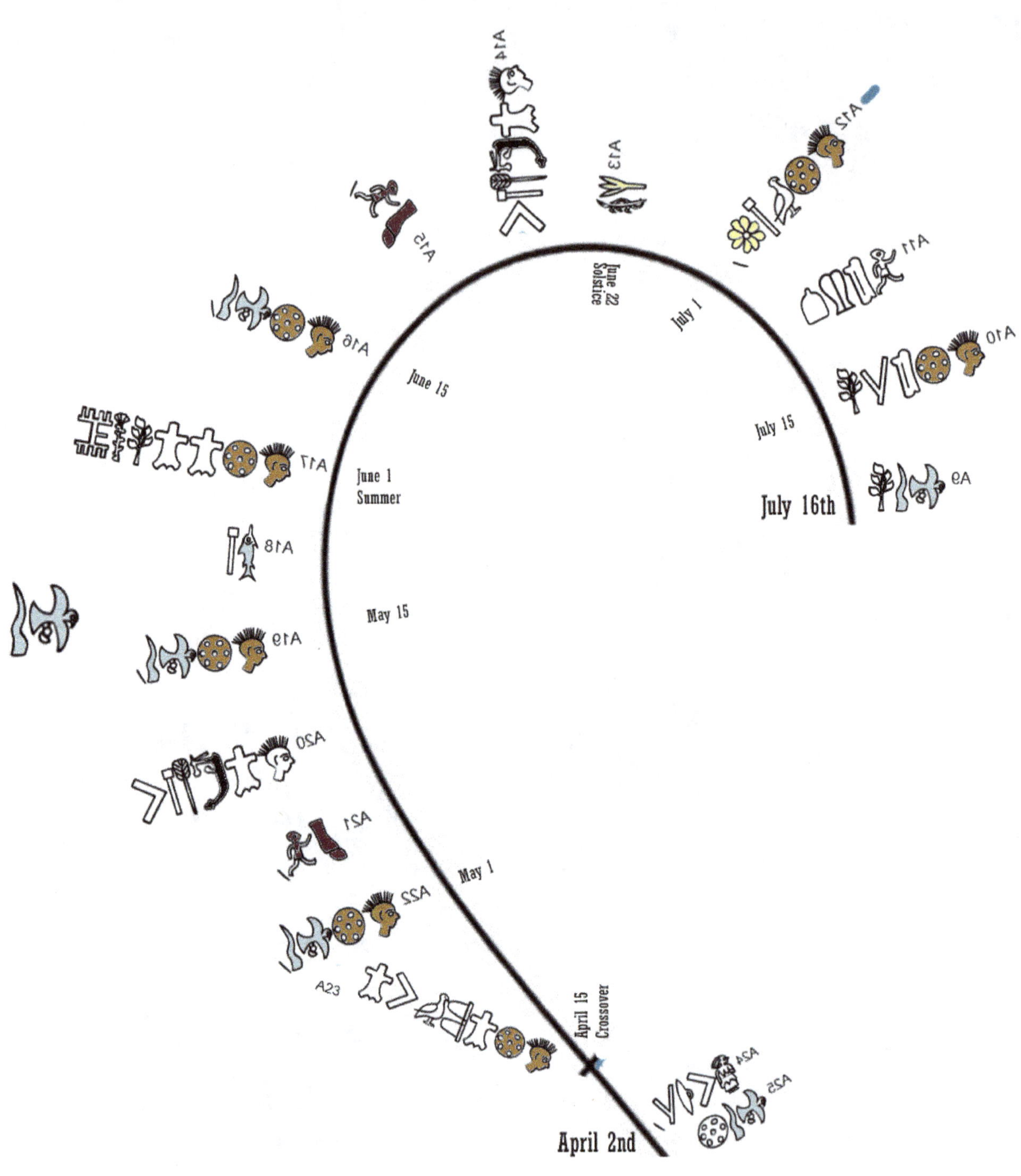

Horn and Bird Symbol Group Coverage.

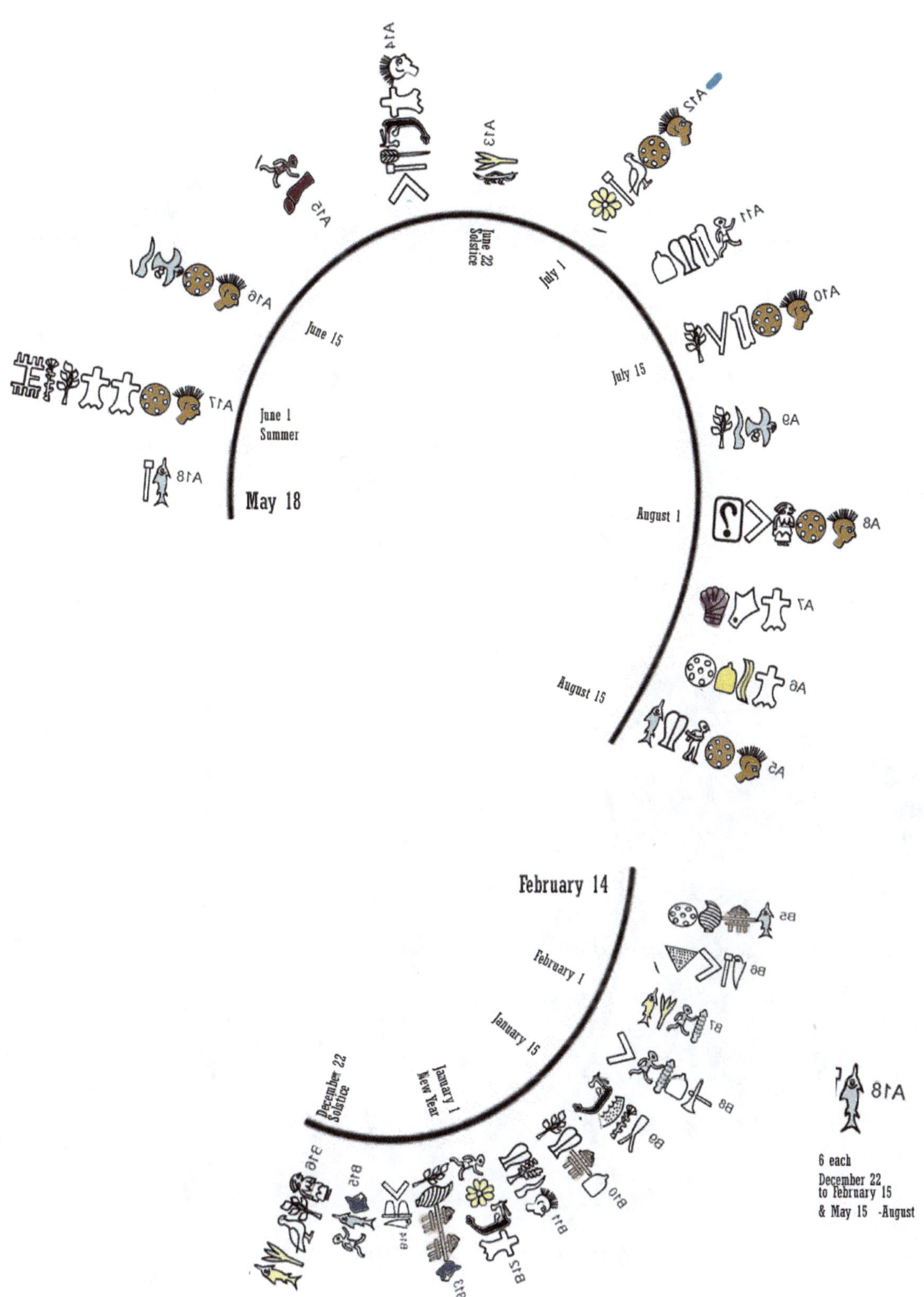

Tuna Symbol Coverage.

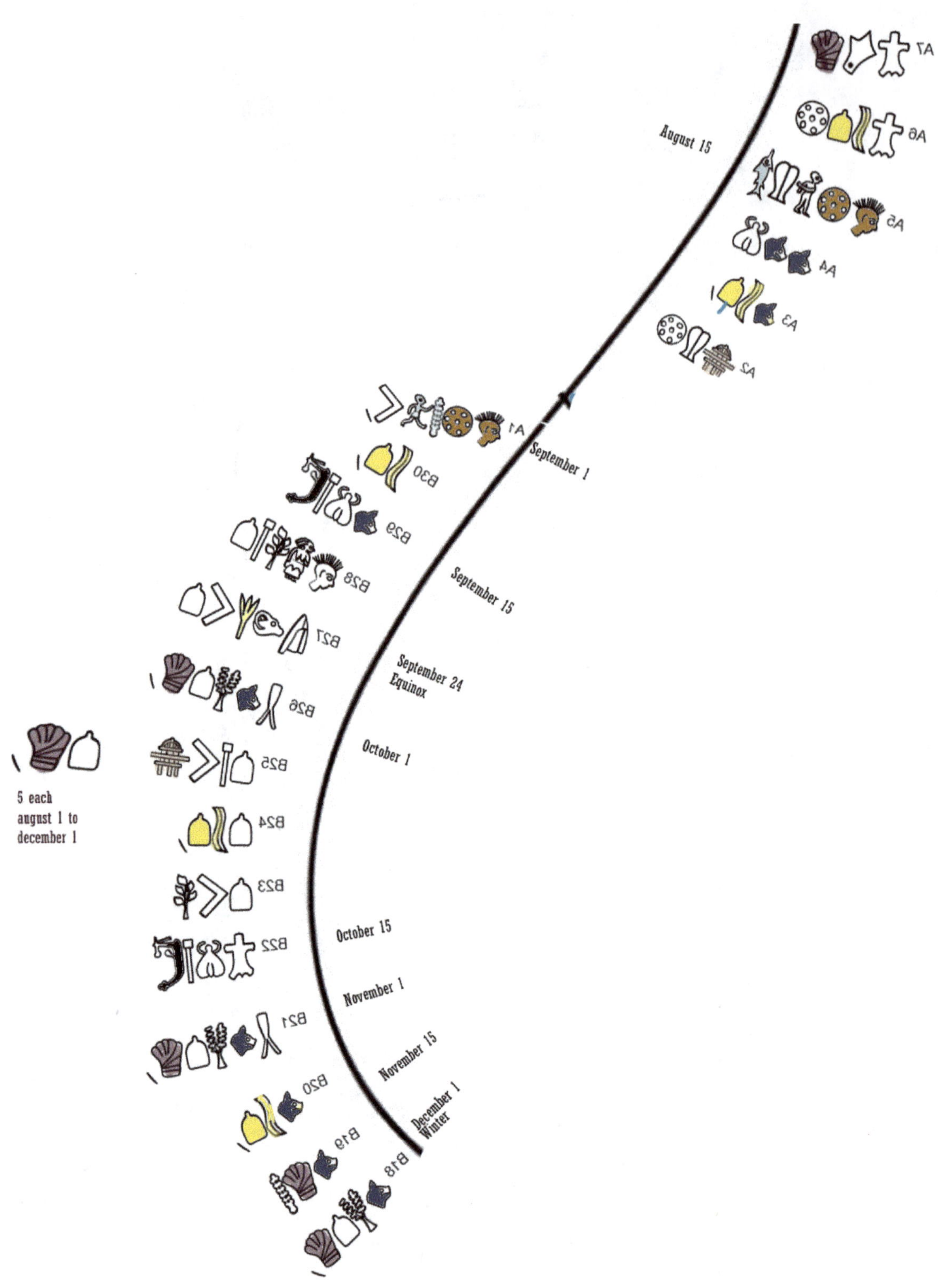

Glove and Helmet Group Coverage.

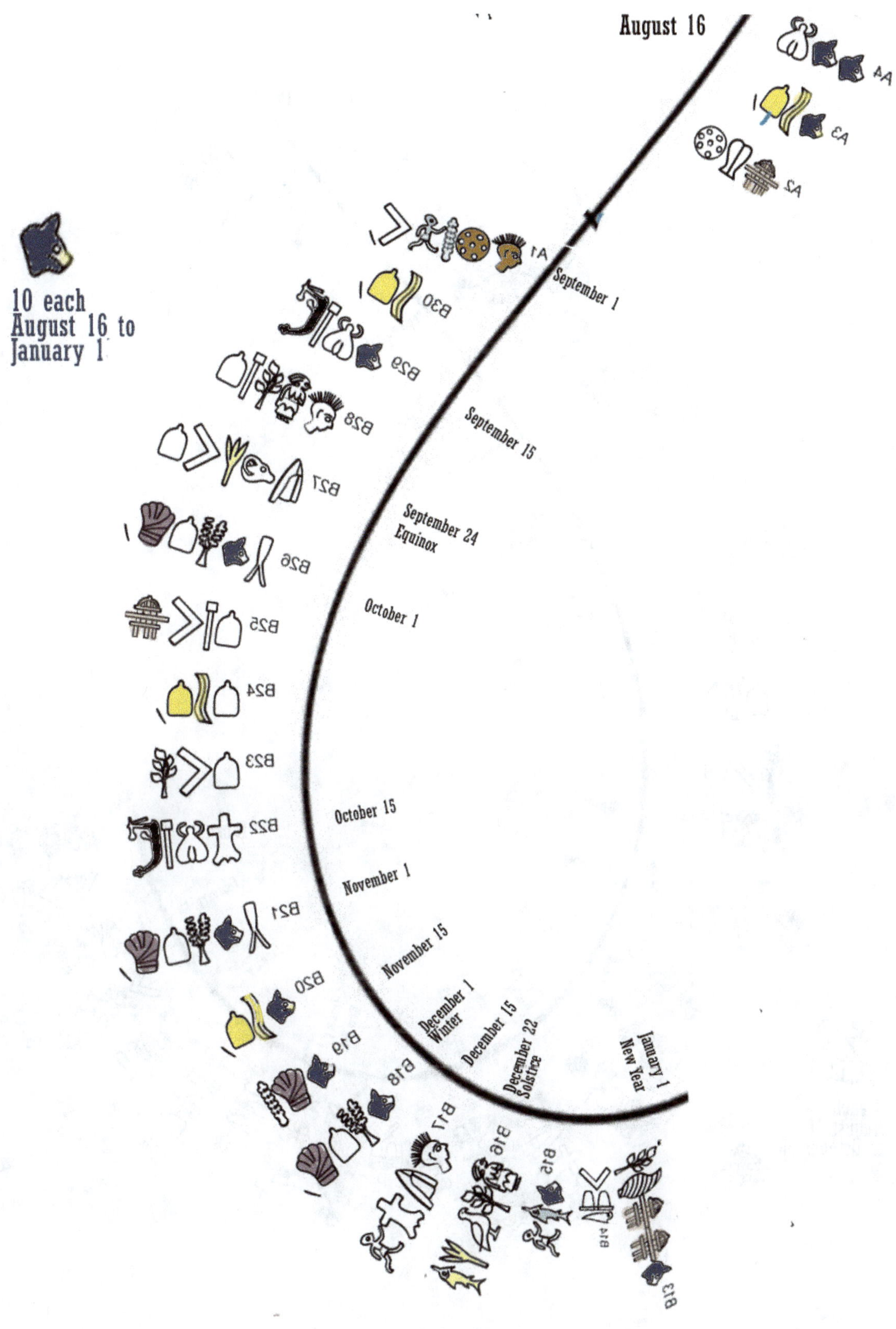

Cat Symbol Coverage.

Chris Hegg

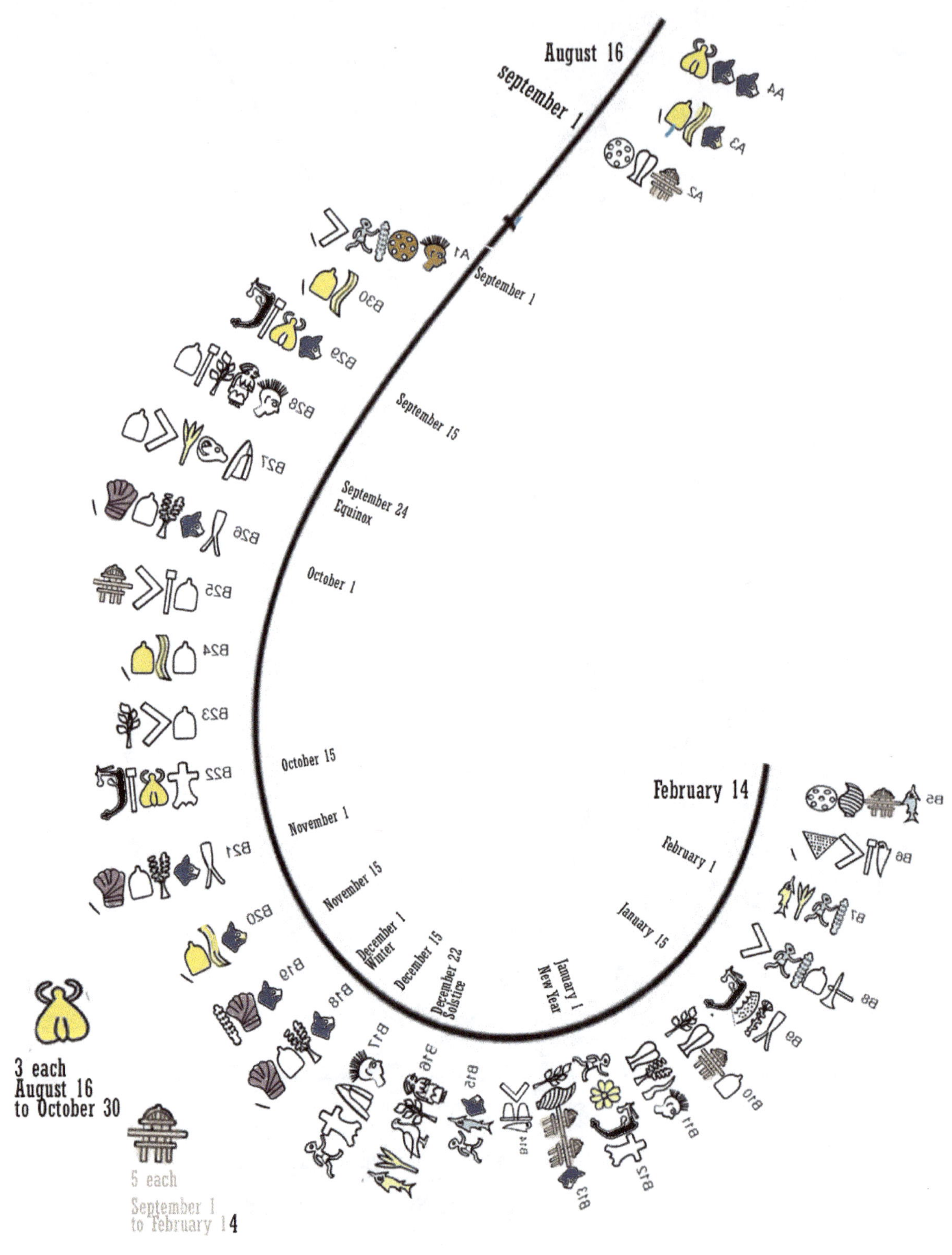

Bee and Hive Symbol Coverages.

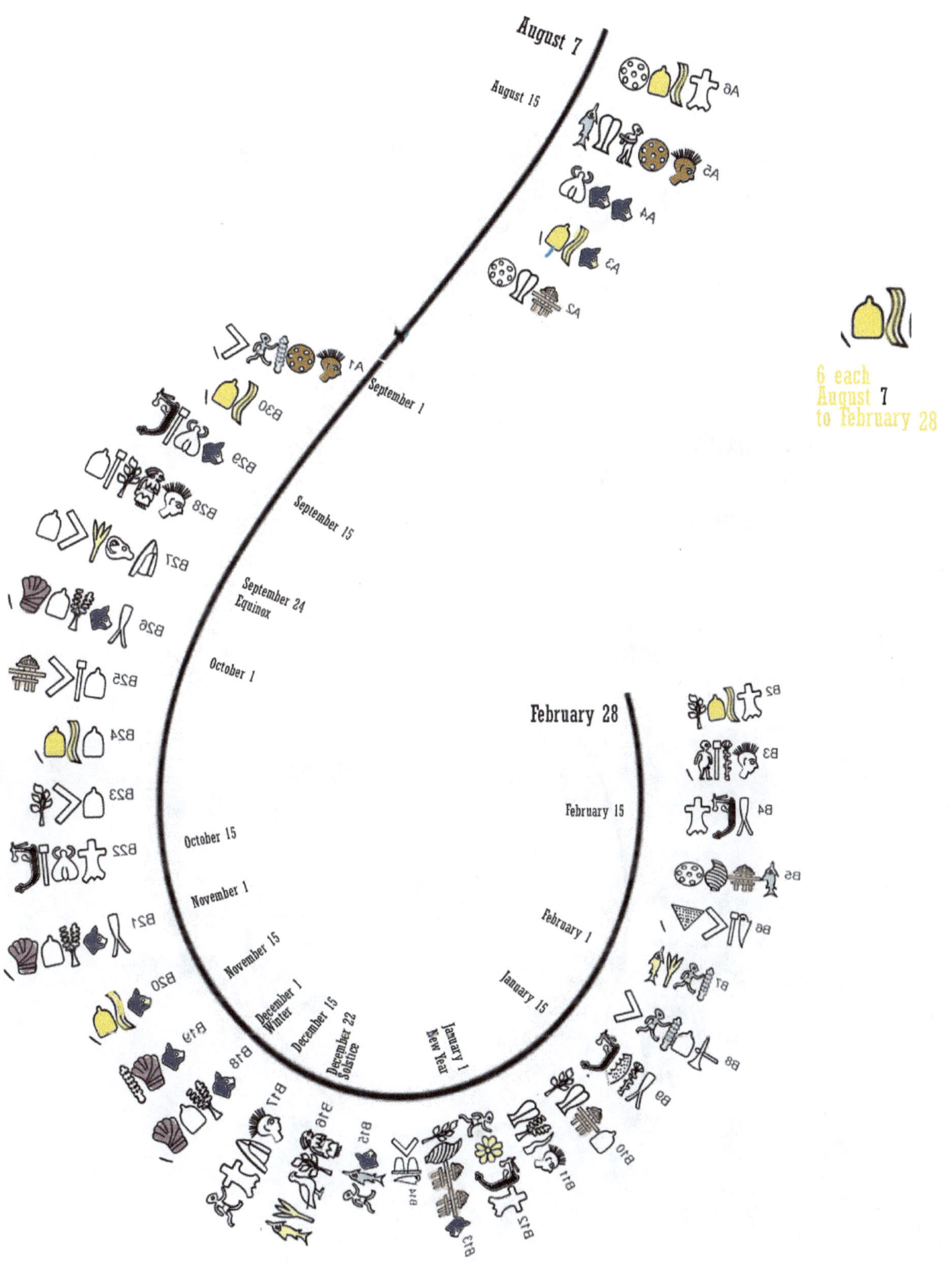

Helmet and Wavy Line Group Coverage.

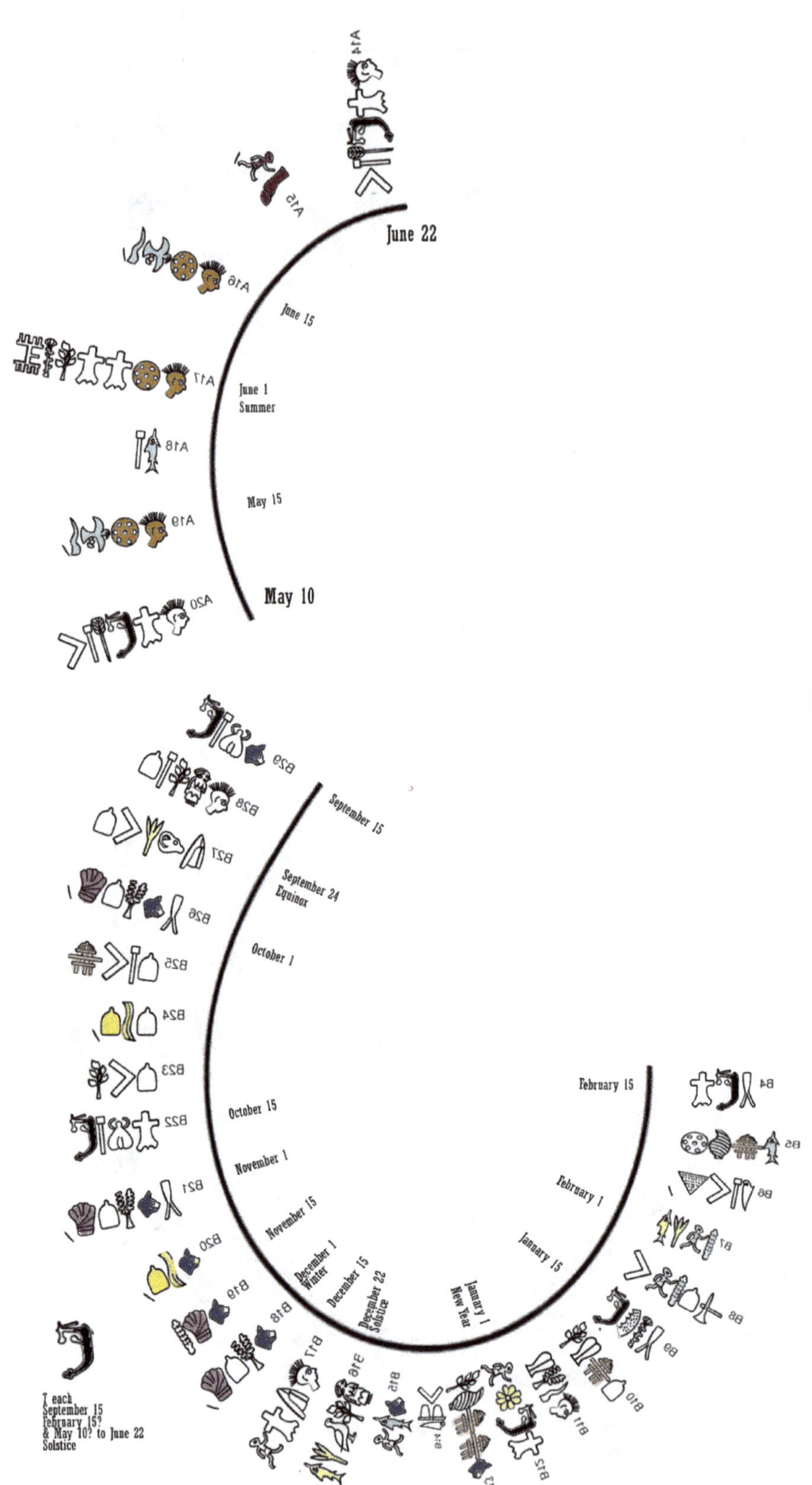

Ship Symbol Coverage.

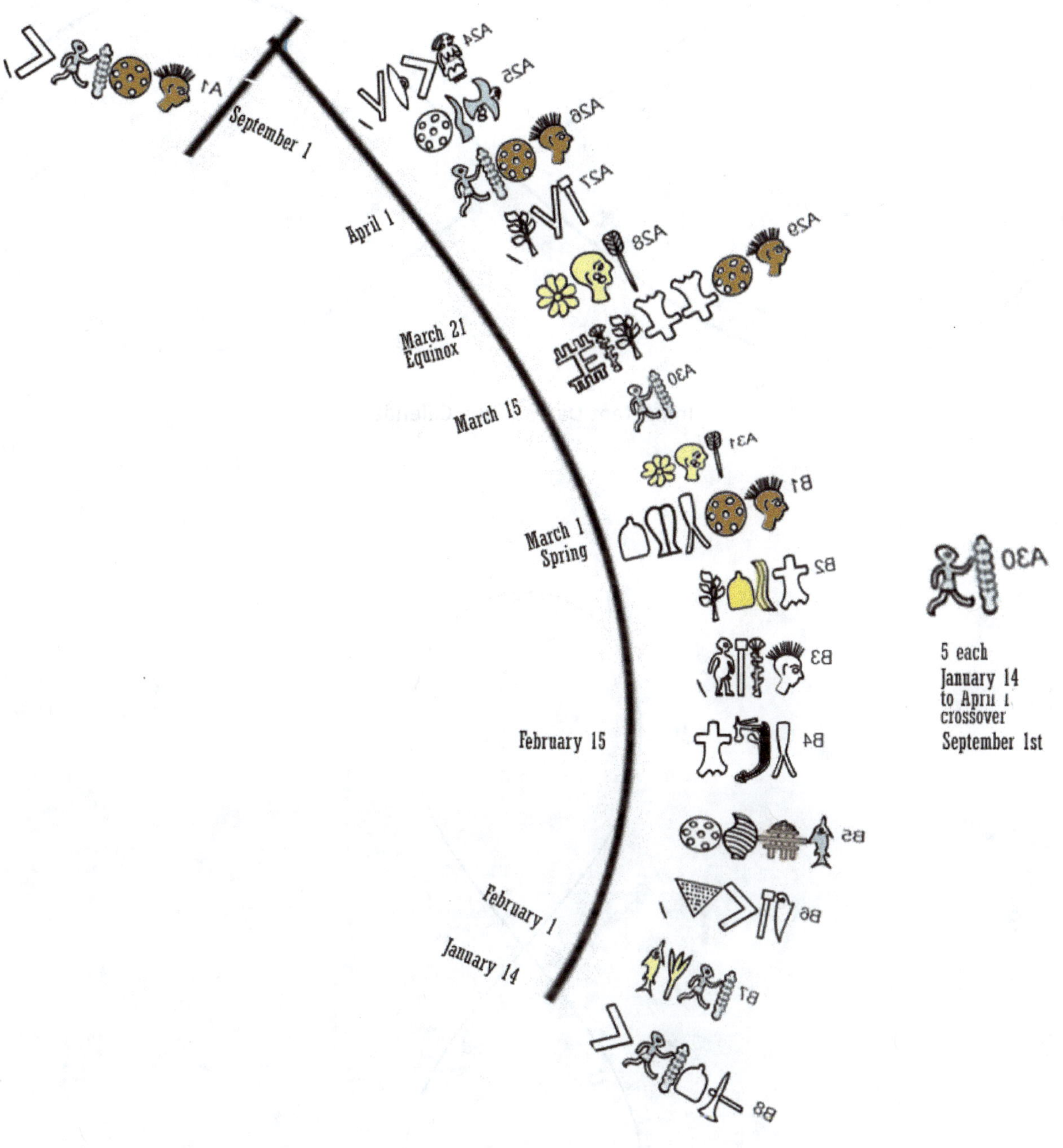

Walking Man and Cane Group Coverage.

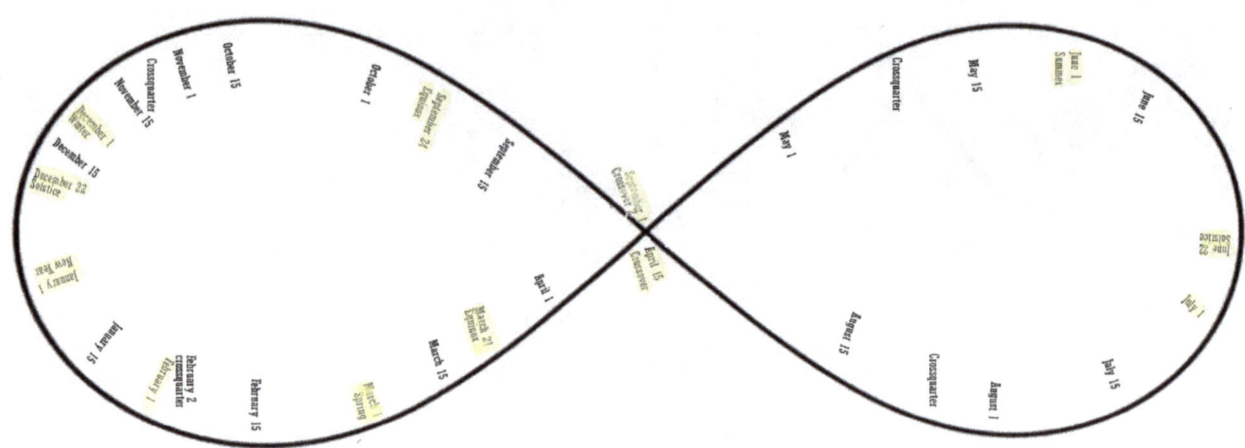

Important Dates of the Calendar.

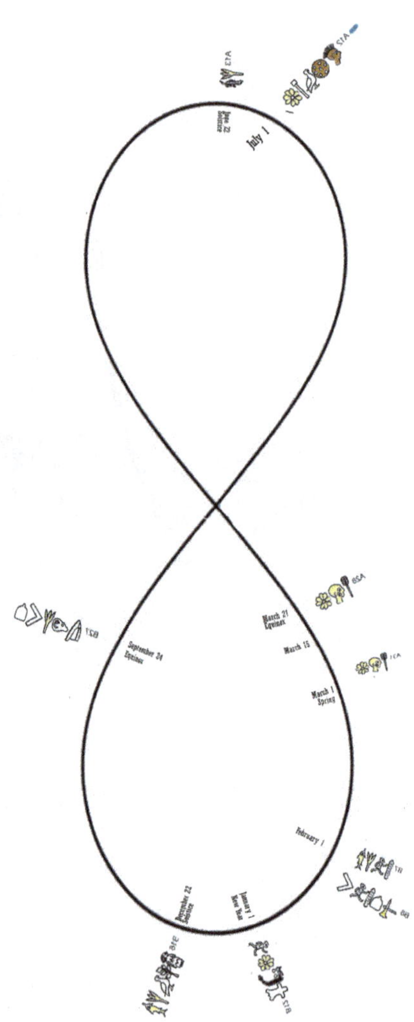

Important Lily and Flower Symbols, Including Axe

Important Symbols and Symbol Groupings Defined

Wagon Wheel and Plume Head Symbol Group on the Phaistos Disc "The Wheel In The Sky Keeps On Turning…"

No symbol group is more critical on the whole of the Phaistos Disc than the wagon wheel and plume head symbol groups. Starting on Side B is the March 1st (B1 group) showing, and it ends on the last symbol group of Side A for September 1st (A1 group), which concludes two days before the second solar crossover.

The vital symbol group designates the fifteen-day months that start in spring on March 1st and end in winter on September 1st. The symbol group always ends the monthly name, assuredly conveying the meaning of "Month."

- Beginning on March 1st (B1 group), the symbols emerge on the calendar.

- March 15th (A29 group), the symbols comprise the largest seven-symbol group on the artifact, which is duplicated identically on June 1st (A17 group) for the summer except for upside-down dual symbols of skins.

- April 1st (A26 group), the symbols merge with the walking man and staff symbol group for the month.

- At the first solar crossover on April 15th (A15 group), the symbols merge with another seven-symbol group comprising a similar pelt configuration to the A29 group and A17 group mentioned as maybe meaning the "half way point" to June 1st summer.

- On May 1st (A22 group), the symbols merge with the horn and bird symbol group.

- May 15th (A19 group) symbols are identical to the A22 group of May 1st.

- June 1st summer (A19 group), the symbols comprise the identical seven-symbol group mentioned on March 15th.

- June 15th (A16 group), the symbols comprise the identical A22 group and A19 group, ending the three similar groups discussed earlier in the horn and bird symbol section.

- July 1st (A12 group): The symbols turn to a six-symbol group for the month's name.

- On July 15th (A10 group), the symbols remain with six symbol groups.

- August 1st (A8 group) maintains a five-symbol group, with the first being damaged and unknown. If the author were to propose what that symbol could be, it is believed to be a glove.

- August 15th (A5 group) maintains a five-symbol group.

- September 1st (A1 group) is the last group, occurring directly before the second solar crossover event.

As a reference, the unique bald head symbol of March 2nd (A28 group) and March 21st spring equinox (A28 group) could somehow correlate to the plumed head.

Crete Ancient Wagon Tracks in Association With the Wagon Wheel Symbol on the Phaistos Disc

This section comprises a possible connection to evidence of a wheel use on Crete.

The ancient possible wagon tracks eroded on Crete provide intriguing insights into the island's historical landscape and transportation networks. Here's a description of these tracks and their significance:

- **Appearance:** The ancient wagon tracks on Crete are visible as shallow, linear depressions or grooves worn into the natural rock or soil surface. These tracks typically form parallel ruts spaced apart to accommodate the width of a wheeled vehicle, such as a cart or wagon. Over time, erosion, weathering, and vegetation growth may have obscured or altered the appearance of these tracks, but their distinctive linear pattern and alignment can still identify them.

- **Location:** The ancient wagon tracks on Crete are found in various locations across the island, including rural areas, coastal plains, and mountainous terrain. They often followed natural pathways and routes that were conducive to wheeled transportation, connecting settlements, agricultural areas, and trade routes. Some tracks may lead to ancient harbors, markets, or administrative centers, reflecting their role in facilitating commerce and communication in ancient Crete.

- **Historical Significance:** The presence of ancient wagon tracks on Crete attests to the island's long history of human occupation and economic activity. These tracks are thought to date back to different periods of antiquity, including the Minoan, Classical, and Roman periods, when wheeled vehicles were used for transportation, agriculture, and trade. The existence of well-worn tracks suggests regular use and maintenance over time, indicating the importance of these routes in ancient Cretan society.

- **Transportation Networks:** The network of ancient wagon tracks on Crete formed an integral part of the island's transportation infrastructure, connecting villages, towns, and cities with agricultural hinterlands, ports, and regional markets. These tracks facilitated the movement of goods, people, and livestock, allowing for the exchange of commodities, ideas, and cultural influences across the island and beyond. They played a crucial role in the development and integration of Cretan communities and economies throughout antiquity.

REFERENCES:
- Cavanagh, William, et al. "Mochlos IIA: Period IV: The Mycenaean Settlement and Cemetery: The Pottery." INSTAP Academic Press, 2013.
- Castleden, Rodney. "Minoans: Life in Bronze Age Crete." Routledge, 2002.
- Schoep, Ilse. "Mochlos IA: Period III: Neopalatial Settlement on the Coast: The Artisans' Quarter and the Farmhouse at Chalinomouri." INSTAP Academic Press, 2005.
- Tzedakis, Yannis. "An Archaeology of Late Antique Pilgrim Flasks." British Archaeological Reports, 2003.

Wheel symbol image from public domain image by author.

Horn and Bird Symbol Group on the Phaistos Disc

The horn and bird symbol group exists on Side A only and consists of five groups covering April 2nd to July 16th. The author considers this symbol group to represent the name of the period between April 1st and July 15th, which brackets the primary tuna run season.

Unique to the disc, the horn and bird symbols merge with the important wagon wheel and plumed head symbol pack for May 1st, May 15th, and June 15th, directly in the center of the first and last horn and bird groups.

It may hold another symbolic meaning, starting around sixteen days after the spring equinox and ending around sixteen days after the summer solstice, in a harmonious placement, putting the spread of these symbols approximately four months prior and four months after the June 1st summer date.

Beginning before the solar crossover, the first horn and bird symbol group will be on April 2nd (A25 group) and will be positioned last in the group.

Note the next A22, A19, and A16 groups are identical.

Next, on May 1st (A22 group), the symbols first appear on the monthly symbol.

Next, on May 15th (A19 group), the symbols first appear on the monthly symbol.

Next, on June 15th (A16 group), the symbols first appear on the monthly symbol.

Lastly, on July 16th (A9 group), the symbols also exist.

Image taken by author from the public domain by the author showing horn and bird symbol grouping with details under the bird and the line off the bottom of the horn with apparent tiny feet on the horn as well. This line shows up precisely in other places with the horn.

Image taken by author from the public domain: a walking man and cane, though the author believes it is a measuring device for sowing seeds or planting implements.

Walking Man and Staff Symbol Group on the Phaistos Disc

The walking man and staff symbol grouping comprises five groups between January 16th and April 1st and covers both Side A and Side B of the disc.

It is one of the unique two-symbol groups spread around the calendar, probably defining it as a prominent meaning for the calendar period. Possibly called a similar name to "crop planting," as one could argue, the symbol group of January 15th (B9 group) holds a symbol the author believes is a showing of a field full of seed rows as dots and side scallops on the symbol as small plants growing.

Beginning on Side B on January 28th or a leap year of 29th (B8 group) appears directly behind the first symbol of the arrow/pointer.

Directly after is February 1st (B7 group), the symbol group resides behind the important tuna and lily symbols of Imbolc.

On March 2nd (A30 group) of Side A, the symbol group stands alone.

On April 1st (A26 group), the symbol group was first in the monthly group.

Not until September 3rd (A1 group) does the symbol reemerge with an arrow in front of the monthly group, showing the possible "continuation" of the winter portion of the analemma.

The one single similar symbol monthly group is displayed again on the second solar crossover of September 3rd that matches the April 1st (A25 group) configuration. It is a unique fact this similar symbol only jumps from the possible location of the first solar crossover date on April 15th that splits that month to the second crossover somehow relates to the crossover festivals and meaning to the civilization only envisioned due to the fantastic crossover events of the solar analemma. An arrow symbol added to the "second group" (A1 group) seems to say 'continued' as several symbols go back to Ancient Universal Language symbology. In contrast, April being split by the first crossover may "put on hold" the final half of the month celebration for the second crossover. If an observer lays out the analemma calendar in months, it is clear there is a four-way point at the crossover, which plays well for the walking man and staff symbol groups doubling up precisely on the analemma. Though it can not be explained why, the fact these two physically distant symbol groups, similar to one another, exist within the confines of both crossovers helps prove the calendar and group positions.

It should be noted that other human figures appear around the calendar with somewhat similar symbols, such as the "podium symbol" and the January 1st walking man and flower. The two walking man and sheep foot symbols in May and June may relate and seem to be spread out in a possible associated way.

Helmet and Wavy Band Symbol Group on the Phaistos Disc

This wavy band is essential as the primary placeholder symbol meaning for the oncoming winter months, ending on the first of spring. Like the cat, the honeybee, the beehive, and the glove and helmet, it resides within the winter band of the analemma. The main difference is that the symbols appear to be present only within the in-between regions between months starting on the 1st and the 15th, appearing to be exactly on the 7th to the 10th, though the author believes they reside on the 10th of each. This importance to the calendar overall is obvious, but why is unknown.

The wavey line symbol only appears in this configuration with the helmet and thus is intricately bound to the group as a whole. The author believes it stands for 'divided' or 'equal/split' as the meaning since it is in the middle of the 1st-14th day months, which is every other month on the calendar. This probably means that it is not a helmet symbol at all.

Except for the ending symbol group (which is a similar design to the first group of A5 on Side A with an extra symbol of a pelt), the symbol packs cover five full months 'centered' between month dates. It is, however, absent from then until the last group (B2 group) right before the March 1st spring monthly symbol.

A reference should be made that the singular helmet symbol does appear more frequently around the calendar, but its further relation is unknown.

Image from public domain: Helmet and wavy band symbol group is from a public source. Note the line under the helmet again, as it appears under and sometimes beside the helmet.

Six groups of the helmet and wavy band symbol group exist in order from around August 14th to February 28th.

About August 14th (A6 group) on Side A is the first of a four-symbol group. The last three symbols match the previous helmet and wavy band grouping of February 28th! This similarity may distinctly mark a leap-year date correction period similar to modern calendars.

The second symbol group is on August 20th (A3 group), where the dual symbols are presented first in line.

Third, the symbols remain as the first in line on about September 10th (B30 group), with a difference in the small line under the helmet off to the front of the group. *It should be noted these are the only two symbols in this group, which only happens six times (6 groups/divisions) in the entire artifact. Specifically, A30 group, A21 group, A18 group, A15 group, A13 group, and it B30 group.*

Fourth, the two appear together on October 10th (B24 group), being first in position with another helmet following the two.

Fifth, they appear together on November 10th (B20 group) again in first position.

The sixth and final appearance is not until the group before the March 1st spring symbols on about February 28th (B2 group), where both symbols have a central position in the group.

Glove and Helmet Symbol Group on the Phaistos Disc

There are five glove and helmet symbol groupings on the artifact. In position from just after August 1st to December 1st, and does appear twice, without the helmet symbol but instead a hatchet symbol once (A7 group) and the other being (B19 group) before the last symbol group, both with unknown exact dates.

The glove and helmet group seems to mirror the other autumn and winter symbol groups, such as the cat, the honeybee, the beehive, the ship and helmet, and the wavy band. *It resides on the start date of those last months of October, November, and December.*

Beginning on Side A, immediately after August 1st (A7 group), the symbol is first in the group.

The second occurrence is on Side B on October 1st (B26 group) as the first in the group.

Third, it appears on November 1st (B21 group) as the first symbol.

Fourth, it appears around November 20th as the middle position in that group.

Fifth and lastly, it appears on December 1st (B18 group) as the first symbol.

The Lily and Flower Symbols and Their Importance On the Phaistos Disc

***ADDITION: The author believes the "flower" is a daffodil icon as they are planted late October and bloom early spring.**

The appearance of the four lily symbols on the Phaistos Disc is one of the most important, being placed on significant solar event dates. Beginning on Side A, the lily appears only once on the June 22 summer solstice.

Physically, it is located on the clay disc where the spirals "crossover" from the inner spiral group to the exterior edge of symbols around the final months of Side A. This corresponds with the June 22 summer solstice alignment and thus is significant proof this correlation was intentionally made.

The lily location is also perfectly set where the final month symbol group ends the Side A reading. The calendar then continues on Side B at the center. This positioning of the lily to the ending of the summer season completes the entire Side A, further proof this correlation was intentionally made. The fact that the ending of Side A further corresponds to the ending of the one loop of the analemma to converge into the second solar crossover event shows the creator of the disc thought out the balanced sides and matching natural events wisely. These two facts provide further compelling evidence that the author is correct in the use of the Phaistos Disc as a calendar.

Image taken by author from public domain Glove and helmet symbol group is from a public source by the author. Note the bottom running line coming off the glove, seen in many instances on certain symbols, is also listed as a separate line away from symbols in some instances. This indicates a use for it on the calendar possibly to show 'start' and 'finish' respectively.

It is also noted that the beginning of September begins just before the second crossover, which is why the September month symbol group (A1 group) is shown as the last symbol on Side A. This assists in maintaining a symmetric appearance and clean start for the center symbols of each side due to space limitations to remain singular. As a note, this month's announcement (groups) at the end of each side will again repeat for Side B as the final group for March 1 is listed last.

The next lily symbol (B27 group) resides on the September 24 autumnal equinox date as the group's third symbol.

The next lily symbol (B16 group) resides on the December 22 winter solstice date and is the second symbol in the group.

The final lily symbol (B7 group) resides on February 1 date and has a similar appearance to the winter solstice grouping (B16) of the lily and tuna. It is theorized the purpose for this similarity is due to the bracketing of the winter solstice and the Imbolc Festival date, which is halfway between the new year and spring (March 1st.)

The fact that the fourth and final lily symbol does not fall again on the spring equinox to be perfectly separated like the first three could be the symbolic harmony of the yearly groupings of dates. The rare lily and flower symbols (of the B12 group, A31 group, A28 group, and A12 group) that reside on important natural divisions of the solar year appear to be divided up for a purpose. The lily on December 21/22 (winter solstice) precedes the flower on January 1st (new year.) The lily again appears on February 1st (Imbolc), followed by the flower on March 1st (spring). The flower is seen again on March 21/22 (spring equinox), preceding the lily on June 22nd (summer solstice) to precede the flower on July 1st.

To sum up this balance, it appears that the December 22 to January 1 difference/gap is symbolic of the June 22 to July 1 difference/gap. The same seems similar to the March 1 flower in the March 21/22 difference/gap.

This puts the fourth and final lily in a position to cover what the author believes is an extraordinary place on the calendar for the Imbolc date of February 1 that brackets four of the most critical points of the year. Being directly in the middle of winter solstice/new year and the "start of the year" spring/spring equinox.

This observation may also be endorsed by the appearance of the axe head symbol on the February 1st B8 group located directly before the lily symbol of Imbolc. This axe, in any account, could signify the 'splitting,' 'division,' or 'separation' of the essential solar dates.

The fact that these four lily symbols match around a calendar analemma to land upon four important bracketed solar events lends credibility to the calendar proposal.

One other essential reference to unique and rare symbols on the Phaistos Disc is the seed planting plot symbol located on January 15 (B9 group), which clearly shows a field with fresh poked holes for seed planting tasks in rows. The edge appears as small leafing plants beyond the seed field. This seed planting is referenced below in the Imbolc Festival history and appears to be presented in the correct order. The next possible seed sprouting symbol present could be what has been called the 'grater' triangle (B6 group) on about February 2nd, which may relate to the seed planting symbol as neither repeats again on the disc.

Background

Throughout history, the lily has held significant symbolism in various cultures, representing purity, beauty, and spirituality. From ancient civilizations to modern societies, the lily's symbolism has endured, evolving and adapting across time and geography. This report explores the ancient meanings of the lily symbol, delving into its cultural significance and enduring legacy.

- **Ancient Egypt:** In ancient Egypt, the lily, particularly the blue lotus (Nymphaea caerulea), held profound religious and cultural significance. Depicted in Egyptian art and hieroglyphs, the blue lotus symbolized rebirth, fertility, and the afterlife. It was associated with the sun god Ra and the creation myth, where the lotus emerged from the primordial waters to symbolize the emergence of life. The blue lotus was also used in religious rituals and funerary practices, including burial rites and temple ceremonies.

- **Ancient Greece:** In ancient Greece, the lily, known as the "Madonna lily" or "Easter lily" (Lilium candidum), was associated with various deities, particularly Hera, the queen of the gods, and Aphrodite, the goddess of love and beauty. The lily symbolized purity, femininity, and motherhood, often depicted in Greek art and mythology. According to legend, the lily originated from the milk of Hera, making it a sacred symbol of motherhood and fertility. The Madonna lily was also used in religious ceremonies and festivals, including weddings and funerals, as a symbol of purity and renewal.

- **Ancient Rome:** In ancient Rome, the lily symbolized prosperity, abundance, and royalty. It was associated with the goddess Juno, the protector of women and marriage, and Venus, the goddess of love and beauty. The lily's elegant beauty and fragrance made it a popular motif in Roman art, architecture, and decorative arts. The Roman aristocracy often adorned their homes and gardens with lilies as a symbol of status and wealth, while religious ceremonies and processions featured lilies as offerings to the gods.

REFERENCES:
- Wilkinson, Richard H. "The Complete Gods and Goddesses of Ancient Egypt." Thames & Hudson, 2003.
- Boardman, John. "The Greeks: A Portrait of Self and Others." Oxford University Press, 2002.
- Beard, Mary, et al. "The Oxford Classical Dictionary." Oxford University Press, 2012.

Lily and flower symbol images by the author from public domain.

Imbolc Holiday Referenced Within the Phaistos Disc (Final Lily Symbol Placement Defined)

Imbolc, as a festival, is primarily associated with Celtic and Gaelic traditions and does not have direct ties to ancient Greece or surrounding ancient societies. The celebration of Imbolc is deeply rooted in Celtic mythology, folklore, and the agricultural practices of the Celtic peoples. The author believes the Imbalc is celebrated in some fashion and listed on the Phaistos Disc (see section lily symbol.)

However, it's worth noting that ancient Greek and neighboring societies had their festivals and rituals that marked the transition from winter to spring. These celebrations often centered around agricultural themes, fertility rites, and the worship of deities associated with renewal and rebirth.

For example, in ancient Greece, the festival of Thesmophoria, dedicated to Demeter, the goddess of agriculture and fertility, was celebrated in the fall, and the harvest and the mysteries of grain fertility were honored. While Thesmophoria does not directly correspond to Imbolc, it shares similarities in its focus on agricultural cycles and seasonal changes.

Similarly, in neighboring ancient societies such as those of Anatolia (modern-day Turkey) and Mesopotamia (modern-day Iraq), there were festivals and rituals dedicated to deities associated with agriculture and fertility. These celebrations often involved offerings, feasting, and rituals aimed at ensuring bountiful harvests and the renewal of life in the spring.

While there may not be a direct connection between Imbolc and ancient Greek or surrounding societies, the themes of renewal, fertility, and the awakening of the Earth are universal. They can be found in various cultures throughout history. As such, while Imbolc may be specific to Celtic traditions, it shares common themes with festivals and celebrations in other ancient societies around the world.

1. Burkert, Walter. "Greek Religion: Archaic and Classical." Harvard University Press, 1985.

2. Parker, Robert. "Miasma: Pollution and Purification in Early Greek Religion." Oxford University Press, 1996.

3. Woolley, Leonard. "Religious Life in Ancient Mesopotamia." Clarendon Press, 2011.Top of Form

Origins

Imbolc celebrated on February 1st, marks the midpoint between the winter solstice and the spring equinox in the Celtic calendar. It is a festival of light, purification, and the awakening of the Earth from its winter slumber. Imbolc is traditionally associated with the goddess Brigid (or Bridget), who embodies aspects of fire, fertility, poetry, and healing in Celtic mythology. The festival holds deep significance in Celtic and pagan traditions, symbolizing the gradual transition from winter darkness to the renewal of life and growth in spring.

- **Origins and Symbolism:** Imbolc derives its name from the Old Irish word "Imbolg," which translates to "in the belly," reflecting the pregnant ewes preparing to give birth at this time of year. The festival marks the beginning of the lambing season and the emergence of new life in nature. Imbolc is also associated with the increasing power of the Sun as the days lengthen and the promise of warmer days ahead.

- **Traditional Practices:** Imbolc is celebrated with various rituals and customs that honor the changing seasons and pay homage to the goddess Brigid. One common tradition is the lighting of candles or bonfires to symbolize the return of light and warmth. Brigid's crosses, woven from rushes or straw, are hung in homes to invoke her protection and blessings. It is also a time for cleansing and purification, with rituals such as spring cleaning, smudging with herbs, and bathing in sacred waters.

- **Brigid and the Hearth:** Brigid plays a central role in Imbolc celebrations, representing the hearth, home, and hearthfire. She is honored as the guardian of the hearth, the keeper of the flame that sustains life and nourishes the soul. Offerings of food, milk, and flowers are made to Brigid to seek her blessings for fertility, abundance, and protection. In some traditions, a special meal is prepared featuring dairy-based dishes such as butter, cheese, and milk, symbolizing the return of life and sustenance.

- **Poetry, Music, and Creativity:** Imbolc is also a time for celebrating creativity, inspiration, and the arts. Poetry, music, storytelling, and other forms of creative expression are embraced as ways to honor Brigid and awaken the dormant energies of winter. *It is a time for setting intentions, making wishes, and planting seeds of new beginnings, both literally and metaphorically.*

- **Modern Celebrations:** In modern times, public gatherings, rituals, workshops, and festivals may be held to celebrate Imbolc and honor the traditions of the past while adapting them to contemporary contexts.

- **Conclusion:** Imbolc is a time of hope, renewal, and anticipation, marking the gradual transition from winter darkness to the promise of spring. Through rituals, customs, and reverence for the goddess Brigid, Imbolc invites a welcoming for the return of light and life to the world.

REFERENCES:
- Kondratiev, Alexei. "The Apple Branch: A Path to Celtic Ritual." Citadel Press, 2003.
- McColman, Carl. "Celebrating the Seasonal Holy Days: A Collection of Seasonal Holy Day Celebrations." New Page Books, 2011.
- Nichols, Ross. "The Book of Druidry." Thorsons, 1990.

The Cat Symbol on the Phaistos Disc

The location of the eleven cat head symbols dominates on the Phaistos Disc, spanning from August 16th to December 31st. This correlates to the coming winter months, terminating at the new year. This may be a leftover symbol with the meaning of an older ten-month calendar that did not track the January-February cycle.

Beginning immediately after the January 15th monthly symbol group, a two-cat group (A4 group) starts the precession of the image, with both cat symbols located last. The very next group holds the next last-position cat symbol on about August 20th (A3 group.)

Next along the calendar after the second solar crossover is the September 15th monthly group (B29 group), where the cat head is listed last again. This concludes the three last position cat symbol groups, which are significant.

Note that the following two listed groups of the B26 group and B21 groups are identical in symbols, as is the B18 group, except it is missing the last symbol of the previous two groups described. All three of these similar groups correspond to October 1st, November 1st, and December 1st, which clearly indicates they have designated these three months. Add this to having a cat symbol present directly preceding August 15th, appearing on September 15th, again on November 15th, and directly before January 1st in different group configurations. There is a solid tie to the start of each month. Also noted is the cat is missing from other months between these dates, but few (September 1st, October 15th, December 15th) and include two non-corresponding dates, the presence of which is between November 18th to 30th and around December 23rd. This indicates some other significant meaning unknown as of this writing.

Next, the symbol appears on the October 1st month symbol (B21 group), where the symbol is fourth.

The following symbol is present in the November 1st monthly group (B21 group) in fourth place.

The next appearance is directly after November 1st (B20 group), possibly on November 10th, and the symbol is in the third location of the group.

Next, and again directly after the last rendition, is the cat in a first-place location on December 1st (B18 group) in the fourth position of the group.

It should be noted that December 1st is the first day of the true season of winter on the calendar, but again, autumn and winter are on the same side of the artifact and possibly called "Winter" as a whole. This could indicate December 1st is the 'middle' of the winter timeframe, or they understood the separate seasons and used two seasons per disc side.

These four-in-a-row groupings displaying the cat symbol indicate something to do with the new season or the halfway point of winter, and all three symbols remaining last in the group again have significant meaning.

After the winter solstice, approximately December 23rd (B12 group), the cat symbol is once again last in the group.

Lastly, on December 31st (B13 group), the final cat symbol resides in last place again.

Noted is that the second of the cat groups (A3 group) is identical to the sixth cat symbol group (B20 group) minus what appears to be a connected 'tail' line under the helmet in the first grouping, which is a disconnected 'tail' line lying beside the helmet symbol in the second.

It is noted that the similarities between groups A3 and B20 extend to two other short groups somewhat divided equally between these (B30 group and B24 group), which maintain the wavy band and helmet symbols in a similar configuration. See the similar-color-coded symbol groups in further images of this divided phenomenon later in this report.

Images from the public domain showing examples of the similarities within the symbol groups discussed. These symbols are in reverse order of actual usage described by the author per group. It should be noted the public domain imagery of symbology does not show slight deviations in designs and uses one icon for all similar symbols, which is somewhat misleading.

- **Background:** Cats have held a significant place in human societies since ancient times. From Egypt to Mesopotamia, Greece, and beyond, cats have been associated with various gods, goddesses, and mythological beings, embodying traits of protection, fertility, and cunning.

- **Ancient Egypt:** In ancient Egypt, cats were revered as sacred animals associated with the goddess Bastet (also known as Bast). Bastet was depicted as a lioness or a woman with the head of a lioness, symbolizing maternal protection, fertility, and feminine power. Cats were believed to embody the essence of Bastet, serving as protectors of homes and temples and guardians against evil spirits and vermin. The ancient Egyptians often depicted cats in art and sculpture, portraying them as graceful and regal creatures worthy of admiration and respect.

- **Mesopotamia:** In Mesopotamian mythology, cats were associated with the goddess Ishtar (also known as Inanna), the goddess of love, fertility, and war. Ishtar was often depicted with lions or lionesses as symbols of her power and authority. Cats were also revered for their ability to hunt and control pests, making them valuable companions in agricultural societies. In Mesopotamian art and literature, cats were depicted as symbols of strength, agility, and cunning, embodying qualities revered by ancient civilizations.

- **Ancient Greece:** In ancient Greece, cats were associated with various deities, particularly the goddess Artemis, the goddess of the hunt, wilderness, and childbirth. Artemis was often depicted with wild animals, including cats, symbolizing her connection to nature and her role as a protector of wildlife. Cats were also associated with other deities, such as Dionysus, the god of wine and revelry, and Hecate, the goddess of magic and witchcraft. In Greek mythology, cats were portrayed as mysterious and independent creatures, embodying traits of cunning and intuition.

Image taken by author from public domain: cat symbol

- **Cultural Legacy:** The symbolism of cats in ancient times continues to resonate in modern society, with cats often depicted as symbols of mystery, independence, and wisdom. From ancient Egyptian artifacts to contemporary literature, art, and popular culture, cats remain enduring symbols of grace, beauty, and resilience. Their enigmatic nature and mysterious behavior continue to fascinate and captivate people around the world, ensuring their place as cherished companions and cultural icons throughout the ages.

REFERENCES:

- Wilkinson, Richard H. "The Complete Gods and Goddesses of Ancient Egypt." Thames & Hudson, 2003.
- Black, Jeremy, and Anthony Green. "Gods, Demons, and Symbols of Ancient Mesopotamia: An Illustrated Dictionary." University of Texas Press, 1992.
- Green, Miranda. "Animals in Celtic Life and Myth." Routledge, 1992.

Bee Symbols on the Phaistos Disc

Bees, like in many other regions, play a vital role in pollination and the ecosystem of Crete, Greece. The activity of bees in Crete follows a seasonal pattern influenced by climate, flora, and other environmental factors.

The bee symbol, starting on Side A of the Phaistos Disc, is not present until near the end of the outer disc, about August 16th (A4 group), and is the first symbol of the group, showing importance. *It will be noted later that the first beehive symbol appears directly after this symbol group (A2 group) just days later.*

The next bee symbol is on the Phaistos Disc Side B, on September 15 (B29 group), but it is the third symbol inward, showing that it is not as important. *It should be noted that this symbol grouping has three distinct symbols similar to those placed in the next discussed group (B29 group and B22 group, respectively) and thus is significant somehow.*

Lastly, the final bee symbol is on October 15 (B22), with the bee symbol being the third symbol.

These three bee symbol groups (A4 on Side A, B29, and B22 on Side B) bracket the first beehive symbols on the disc, denoting a possible connection to their meaning. This late in the year, starting the autumn season, possibly shows the preparation of natural food storage within the hives. At the same time, bee activity still somewhat exists in preparation for winter and the process of bees and honey by nature and by man to maintain the hives.

The significance of both the bee symbols and the beehive symbols corresponding to the same proximity to one another on the calendar year and their usage proposed in this paper further solidifies the analemma and season bracketing outlined.

Though both symbols are essential in civilization, it is believed these two symbols do not designate a defined beginning or ending to the object's calendar seasons or months. Thus, they only hold a reference to an industry they are dependent upon as inclusive to the calendar.

Bee Background

Here's a general description of the active days of bees in Crete:

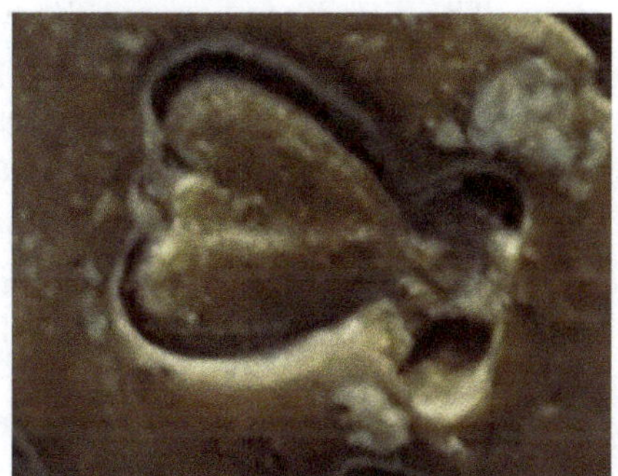

Image taken by author from public domain: bee symbol

- **Spring:** In spring, typically from March to May, bees in Crete become increasingly active as temperatures rise and flowers bloom. This period marks the start of the beekeeping season, as bees begin foraging for nectar and pollen to feed their colonies and rear brood. With the abundance of flowering plants and trees, including citrus orchards, wildflowers, and olive groves, bees have ample resources to collect and sustain their colonies. Beekeepers in Crete often harvest early spring honey, characterized by its light color and delicate flavor, during this time.

- **Summer:** Summer, from June to August, is the peak of bee activity in Crete. With warm temperatures and long daylight hours, bees are highly active in foraging and honey production. The island's diverse vegetation, including herbs such as thyme, sage, and oregano, as well as flowering trees like chestnuts and eucalyptus, provide abundant sources of nectar and pollen for bees to collect. Beekeepers manage their hives carefully during this period, ensuring that colonies have sufficient space and resources to thrive. Summer honey harvested in Crete is prized for its rich flavor and aromatic qualities, often reflecting the unique floral sources of the island.

- **Autumn:** As autumn arrives, typically from September to November, bee activity in Crete gradually begins to decline. While temperatures remain relatively warm, flowering plants become less abundant, signaling the end of the foraging season. Bees focus on gathering resources to prepare for winter, storing honey and pollen in their hives to sustain them through the colder months ahead. Beekeepers may conduct hive inspections and preparations for overwintering during this time, ensuring that colonies are healthy and well-provisioned for the coming season.

- **Winter:** In winter, from December to February, bee activity in Crete decreases significantly as temperatures drop and floral resources become scarce. Bees form winter clusters within their hives to conserve heat and maintain their colonies' temperature. While some foraging may still occur on milder days, beekeeping activities are minimal during this time. Beekeepers may provide supplemental feeding to ensure that colonies have enough food to survive until spring.

Overall, the active days of bees in Crete follow the seasonal rhythms of nature, with peak activity occurring during spring and summer when floral resources are abundant. Beekeepers play a crucial role in managing hives and harvesting honey, supporting both the bee population and agricultural ecosystems on the island.

REFERENCES:

- Papanastasiou, Ioannis, et al. "Beekeeping in Crete." Bee World, vol. 86, no. 4, 2005, pp. 95-102.
- Sgardelis, Stefanos P., et al. "The Role of Honeybees (Apis mellifera L.) in Pollination and Conservation of Mediterranean Ecosystems: A Review." Journal of Apicultural Research, vol. 53, no. 4, 2014, pp. 425-437.

Beehive Symbols on the Phaistos Disc

The beehive symbols begin around August 25 (A2 group) on Side A of the disc, represented last in the three-symbol group. *This first hive symbol, again, corresponds to the first bee symbol displayed just two groupings before this. The connection due to proximity cannot be overlooked.* The fact that this beehive symbol is last in the group is also significant.

The next beehive symbol is on Side B around October 1-5th (B25 group), with the emblem being first in the group. The difference between the two groups having last- and first-placed symbols in their respective groupings could indicate the precession expressed in the calendar year location, possibly waning with age or activity/importance of the hive as time passes into colder months.

The beehive symbol reemerges as a double symbol on December 30 (B13 group), where it has two hives together in locations three and four, having possible meaning for the new year immediately after. This dual hive occurrence lining up with the new year/end-of-year date is another compelling marker for proof of the disc as a calendar. These double symbols are present within the center of the grouping.

The beehive symbol appears on a January 10th approximate date (B10 group), holding a third placemark location. The next and final beehive symbol appears around February 10 (B5 group), still maintaining a third position within the group, and is the last of the symbols.

The possibility that the beehive symbol location will adjust from last place in August (A2 group) to last place in October (B25 group) coincides with the direction or flow of colder months in the proposed calendar year. Adding to this, the seasons most needed for hives to hold over bees would be Autumn through Winter, which further fits the general symbol locations. Having the dual symbol group at the new year mark (B13 group) additionally justifies the proper importance of the new year mark of the proposed calendar. Lastly, maintaining a third symbol position within the respective groups for the final three groupings (B13, B10, B5) could further solidify the proper placement and order of importance for the symbol usage and relate to the symbol's wanting months.

Beehive symbol is from the public domain image by the author.

Shoulder Yokes Carrying Amphora/Pithos in Relation to the Phaistos Disc

The symbol observed within the A23 and B14 groupings of what is generally considered to represent a yoke for subduing prisoners is, instead, a shoulder yoke carrying two clay amphora vessels. This observation is further supported by the vessel's rounded sides and flat bottoms with the explicit representations of the vessel's rounded lips caught within the yoke's grasp on either side.

This yoke symbol is only present between December 22 and January 1 (B14 group) on the calendar and on the first crossover/April 15 month (A23 group), of which both symbol locations hold significant positions within the calendar year. With only two representations, this report will now describe a brief history of the yoke and a few possible interpretations.

The author, C Hegg, felt compelled to observe the nature of the yoke after once donning a similar type at a colonial fair. Hegg quickly understood the importance of balancing the two sides down to the ounce, or one would soon fall exhausted from the effort of the offset burden. Hegg then pondered the possibility that this yoke does not denote absolute balance in nature, rather, it represents the balance between the winter solstice and the new year, and the balance between April 1 and March 1 as the Sun crosses over its path on March 15, thus completing a voyage of halfway to summer and summer solstice.

The thought of filled storage vessels in motion may also indicate the necessity of food stores to provide throughout winter and until the spring crops that were planted began yielding their harvest.

- **Background:** The connection between solar calendars and human shoulder yokes carrying pithoi in ancient cultures is an intriguing topic that may have various interpretations and potential connections. Here's one possible perspective:

- **Symbolism of Sun and Harvest:** In some ancient cultures, the Sun was revered as a symbol of life, fertility, and agricultural abundance. Solar calendars were developed to track the Sun's movements and mark significant agricultural events such as planting, harvesting, and seasonal changes. The shoulder yokes used to carry pithoi, large storage jars often filled with agricultural products like grain, wine, or oil, could be seen as tools associated with agricultural labor and the harvest cycle. If so, they may designate in my interpretation a showing of carrying over, or storing, the excess foods needed to survive the long winter and to bring in the new year. As the Phaistos Disc two representations of the Shoulder Yokes with Pithos are represented on the New Year of January first, and the first solar crossover of April fifteenth, these representations may describe such reverence.

Shoulder yoke with amphoras image from public domain image by author.

- **Ceremonial Processions and Rituals:** In societies where solar calendars played a significant role, ceremonial processions and rituals were often conducted to celebrate important agricultural milestones or religious festivals linked to the Sun. The act of carrying pithoi on shoulder yokes may have been part of such processions, symbolizing the transportation of harvested goods and offerings to sacred sites or communal gathering places.

- **Alignment with Solar Events:** The timing of these processions and rituals could have been coordinated with key solar events, such as solstices, equinoxes, or other points on the solar calendar. For example, the carrying of pithoi on shoulder yokes may have been performed during the winter solstice, marking the time storage must be maintained from the prior agricultural season to provide abundance to all. The first solar crossover may be listed as the second icon showing the ending or termination of such supplies as new harvests begin to emerge.

- **Cultural and Symbolic Significance:** The act of carrying pithoi on shoulder yokes may have held deeper cultural and symbolic significance beyond its practical purpose. It could have symbolized the collective effort of the community in agricultural activities, the importance of honoring the Sun as a provider of life, or the connection between human labor and the cycles of nature.

- **Archaeological Evidence and Interpretation:** While direct evidence linking shoulder yokes carrying pithoi to solar calendars may be limited, archaeological findings such as depictions in ancient art, inscriptions, or ritual objects could provide clues to understanding the cultural context and symbolism surrounding these practices.

Bluefin Tuna Migration in Association with Symbol Placement on the Phaistos Disc

The depictions of the six tuna symbols on the Phaistos Disc have a single predominantly independent symbol at around May 20th Side A (A18 group) that fits within the calendar cycle, which corresponds to the first day of summer.

The second tuna symbol (A5 group) presents itself first in the group on August 15 as part of the month group. This corresponds with the run of the bluefin tuna and possibly more varieties, as described below.

It is listed as the next iteration on the calendar of the symbol Side B (B16 group) on December 22, winter solstice as the second symbol in the group. *This shows a significant standing being listed at or near both the summer and solstice dates, and the tuna is also present with the renewal symbol of the lily.*

The tuna symbol is listed as the very next symbol group in the second spot in the group (A15 group) after solstice (December 23-25th possibly).

The following calendar tuna symbol is present on the February 1st date as the first symbol (B7 group) is *present with the renewal symbol of the lily.*

The last iteration is present soon after on the calendar, around or before February 15th (B5 group) as the last one in the group. The symbol does not reappear until the summer section of the calendar.

This division in the calendar could coincide with the fishing cycles. In contrast, the primary single symbol and secondary symbol (June 1 to August 15) related to the significant tuna runs as they headed northward. The winter symbol division (December 22 to February 14-15) corresponds to southerly tuna runs that were further out from Crete.

Tuna Background

The migration dates of bluefin tuna near Crete can vary depending on factors such as water temperature, prey availability, and oceanographic conditions. However, typically, bluefin tuna migration patterns in the Mediterranean Sea follow a seasonal cycle. Here's a general overview:

Image taken by author from public domain: tuna symbol

- **Spring Migration (March-May):** During the spring months, bluefin tuna begin their northward migration from their wintering grounds in the southern Mediterranean or Atlantic Ocean. As water temperatures rise and daylight hours increase, tuna move towards cooler and more productive feeding grounds in northern waters, including areas near Crete.

- **Summer Residence (June-August):** In the summer months, bluefin tuna can be found in the waters surrounding Crete and throughout the Mediterranean Sea. These warm months are characterized by increased feeding activity as tuna prey on abundant populations of smaller fish, squid, and other marine organisms. The waters near Crete provide important foraging habitat for bluefin tuna during this time.

- **Autumn Migration (September-November):** As autumn approaches and water temperatures begin to cool, bluefin tuna start their southward migration towards warmer waters for winter. Tuna may pass through the waters near Crete during this period as they return to their wintering grounds in the southern Mediterranean or Atlantic Ocean.

- **Winter Residence (December-February):** During the winter months, bluefin tuna inhabit southern Mediterranean waters or migrate further south to escape colder temperatures. While tuna sightings near Crete may be less common during this time, some individuals or smaller populations may still remain in the region if conditions are favorable.

- **Economic Importance:** The tuna runs near Crete have significant economic implications for local communities, particularly those involved in commercial fishing and tourism. Tuna fishing is a traditional activity in the region, providing livelihoods for fishermen and supporting the local economy. The abundance of tuna during migration seasons attracts commercial fishing fleets and recreational anglers to the area, boosting tourism and generating revenue for businesses.

- **Cultural Heritage:** Tuna fishing has a long history and cultural significance in Crete, dating back to ancient times. Traditional fishing techniques, such as purse seining and trolling, have been practiced by Cretan fishermen for generations. Tuna runs are celebrated at local festivals and events, highlighting the cultural heritage and culinary traditions associated with tuna fishing and consumption on the island.

- The tuna runs near Crete are a natural phenomenon where large schools of tuna migrate through the waters surrounding the island. These tuna runs occur seasonally, typically during the warmer months, and have significant ecological, economic, and cultural importance. Here's a description of the tuna runs near Crete:

- **Migration Patterns:** Tuna, particularly bluefin tuna (Thunnus thynnus), follow specific migration patterns in the Mediterranean Sea, including the waters near Crete. These migrations are influenced by factors such as water temperature, prey availability, and breeding cycles. Tuna typically migrate from their wintering grounds in warmer southern waters to more temperate or cooler northern waters during the spring and summer months.

REFERENCES

- Block, Barbara A., et al. "Tracking apex marine predator movements in a dynamic ocean." Nature 475.7354 (2011): 86-90.
- Karachle, Paraskevi K., et al. "A review of bluefin tuna (Thunnus thynnus) aquaculture: a case study from the Mediterranean Sea." Reviews in Aquaculture 12.1 (2020): 256-277.
- Karakulak, Saadet, and Okan Akyol. "Recent occurrence of the Atlantic bluefin tuna, Thunnus thynnus (Linnaeus, 1758), in Turkish waters of the eastern Mediterranean Sea." Journal of Applied Ichthyology 24.1 (2008): 113-115.

Ship Symbol in Relation to the Tuna Symbol on the Phaistos Disc

The ship is a secondary symbology that is possibly related to the tuna symbols, and thus, the tuna runs in relation to fishing. These fishing trips chasing tuna runs could coincide with the ship symbol placement.

Shipping was a vital part of Crete, and thus, observing the placement of the ship symbols around the calendar analemma suggests that they may be related to tuna fishing and tuna runs of the seasons.

Specifically, of the seven ship symbols present, they are divided around the calendar near the tuna symbols specifically.

Unique to the entire artifact, a repeating of different symbol groups occurring in this section that is inclusive to the ship symbol on Side A that brackets the true start of summer on June 1st. These are the walking man and lamb hoof group A21 (May 7-8th timeframe) followed by the ship group A20 (May 10th timeframe) followed by summer June 1st date and then a repeating walking man and lamb hoof group A15 (June 18th timeframe) ending in the ship group A14 on June 20th. As the tuna symbol group A18 falls between just before summer June 1st the author believes these symbols to be connected, possibly as the 'summer tuna run fishing' dates.

The first ship symbol encountered is directly before the first tuna symbol listed on Side A around June 1 on approximately May 10-15th.

This ship symbol on about May 10th (A20) is identical in symbol type and group as the next iteration of the ship symbol on approximately June 20st (A14 group). Both symbol groups have the ship centrally located in the symbol pack. Note this comprises two of only a few six symbol large symbol groups on the disc as a whole.

The ship symbol does not show up again until the more congested ship groupings on Side B of the Phaistos Disc.

The ship symbol appears on September 15 (B29 group) *possibly representing the start of longer fishing trips to capture*

Image taken by suthor from public domain: ship symbol

the southern migration due to the fact both of the B29 and B22 groups have the ship symbol displayed as the first symbol, showing possible importance.

The next calendar occurrence of the ship symbol is October 15 (B22 group), which concludes the year.

The ship symbol occurs again on January 1 New Year (B12 group) which displays an important grouping and significant place beside the new year flowering bloom. Though the ship is located third in the symbol group instead of the first symbol.

The ship symbol promptly shows up again on January 15 (B9 group) and it is represented as the first symbol, showing a possible importance to this date.

Lastly the ship symbol appears in a center position in the group on the calendar February 15 (B4 group) as the last group present, possibly showing the end of the farther tuna trips until they return during summer. It should be noted the tuna symbol does not appear again.

Important Seasonal Events

Ancient Greek Origins of Solar Calendar Festivals

The festivals of ancient Greece were deeply intertwined with the cycles of nature, particularly those governed by the movements of the Sun. These festivals, marking solstices, equinoxes, cross-quarters, and other solar calendar events, held profound significance in Greek religious, cultural, and agricultural practices. Rooted in ancient beliefs and rituals, these celebrations honored deities, celebrated the changing seasons, and provided communities with a sense of connection to the cosmos. This report will now explore the origins, dates, names, and references of key solar calendar festivals in ancient Greece.

1. Winter Solstice:

Festival Name: Lenaia **Date:** Around December 25th **Description:** Lenaia was a festival dedicated to Dionysus, the god of wine, fertility, and revelry. It marked the rebirth of Dionysus and the promise of the return of life and vegetation with the lengthening of daylight hours after the winter solstice. **Reference:** Burkert, Walter. "Greek Religion: Archaic and Classical." Harvard University Press, 1985.

2. Spring Equinox:

Festival Name: Anthesteria **Date:** Around March 11th to 13th **Description:** Anthesteria was a three-day festival in honor of Dionysus, celebrating the arrival of spring and the maturation of wine. The first day, Pithoigia, involved the opening of jars of new wine. The second day, Choes, was marked by drinking competitions and feasting. The third day, Chytroi, included offerings to the dead. **Reference:** Parker, Robert. "Miasma: Pollution and Purification in Early Greek Religion." Oxford University Press, 1996.

3. Summer Solstice:

Festival Name: Kronia **Date:** Around June 21st **Description:** Kronia was a festival dedicated to Cronus, the god of time and agriculture. It celebrated the height of summer and the bountiful harvest season. During Kronia, social norms were temporarily relaxed, and slaves were allowed to participate in the festivities alongside their masters.

Reference: Burkert, Walter. "Homo Necans: The Anthropology of Ancient Greek Sacrificial Ritual and Myth." University of California Press, 1986.

4. Autumn Equinox:

Festival Name: Eleusinian Mysteries **Date:** Around September 21st **Description:** The Eleusinian Mysteries were a series of secret rites and ceremonies held annually in Eleusis, dedicated to Demeter and Persephone. These mysteries celebrated the cycle of life, death, and rebirth, and offered initiates the promise of a blessed afterlife.

Reference: Kerenyi, Karl. "Eleusis: Archetypal Image of Mother and Daughter." Princeton University Press, 1991.

5. Cross-Quarter Days:

Festival Name: Panathenaea **Date:** Around July 23rd and February 8th **Description:** The Panathenaea were the annual Athenian festivals held in honor of the goddess Athena. The Greater Panathenaea, held every four years, included grand processions, athletic competitions, and cultural events. The Lesser Panathenaea occurred annually and involved sacrifices, feasting, and musical performances.

Reference: Neils, Jenifer. "The Parthenon Frieze." Cambridge University Press, 2001.

Conclusion:

Ancient Greek solar calendar festivals were pivotal in the cultural, religious, and agricultural life of the civilization. They provided communities with opportunities for communal celebration, religious devotion, and connection to the natural world. Rooted in ancient beliefs and rituals, these festivals influence modern traditions and cultural practices.

REFERENCES:

- Burkert, Walter. "Greek Religion: Archaic and Classical." Harvard University Press, 1985.
- Parker, Robert. "Miasma: Pollution and Purification in Early Greek Religion." Oxford University Press, 1996.
- Burkert, Walter. "Homo Necans: The Anthropology of Ancient Greek Sacrificial Ritual and Myth." University of California Press, 1986.

Greek Easter Holiday Carnival

The Greek Easter holiday, known as "Pascha" or "Πάσχα" in Greek, is one of the most important religious and cultural celebrations in Greece. While the actual date of Easter varies each year according to the lunar calendar, it generally falls between late March and late April. The Greek Easter holiday encompasses a series of religious rituals, traditions, and festivities that span several weeks, culminating in a joyous and vibrant celebration.

- **Preparation and Lent:** The Greek Easter season begins with the Great Lent, a period of fasting, repentance, and spiritual preparation that lasts for forty days. During this time, many Greeks abstain from meat, dairy, and other animal products, opting for a diet of seafood, vegetables, and fasting-friendly foods. The Lenten period encourages reflection, prayer, and acts of charity, preparing believers for the solemnity and significance of Easter.

- **Holy Week:** The climax of the Greek Easter season is Holy Week, known as "Megali Evdomada" or "Μεγάλη Εβδομάδα" in Greek. Holy Week begins with Palm Sunday, commemorating Jesus' triumphant entry into Jerusalem. Orthodox Christians attend church services throughout the week, participating in rituals such as the reading of the Twelve Gospels on Thursday evening and the symbolic washing of feet on Holy Thursday.

- **Good Friday and Holy Saturday:** Good Friday, or "Megali Paraskevi" in Greek, is a day of mourning and reflection, commemorating the crucifixion and death of Jesus Christ. Many Greeks participate in solemn processions, carrying symbolic epitaphs adorned with flowers through the streets of their communities. On Holy Saturday, known as "Megalo Sabbato" in Greek, Orthodox Christians attend late-night church services, culminating in the midnight Resurrection liturgy.

- **Easter Sunday:** Easter Sunday, or "Kyriaki tou Paskha" in Greek, is the most joyous day of the Greek Easter holiday. Orthodox Christians celebrate the resurrection of Jesus Christ with fervor and jubilation. The midnight Resurrection liturgy gives way to the "Anastasi" (Ανάσταση), the moment when the priest proclaims "Christos Anesti" (Χριστός Ανέστη), meaning "Christ is risen," and parishioners respond with "Alithos Anesti" (Ἀληθῶς ἀνέστη), meaning "Truly, He is risen." This proclamation marks the beginning of a joyous feast, with families gathering to share a festive meal, including traditional dishes such as "Magiritsa" (Μαγειρίτσα) and "Tsoureki" (Τσουρέκι), a sweet Easter bread.

- **Post-Easter Celebrations:** The Greek Easter holiday extends beyond Easter Sunday, with celebrations continuing throughout the following week. Families and friends gather for picnics, barbecues, and outings, enjoying the springtime weather and festive atmosphere. Traditional Greek music and dance often accompany these gatherings, adding to the sense of joy and community spirit.

In conclusion, the Greek Easter holiday is a vibrant and meaningful celebration that blends religious observance with cultural traditions. It is a time of spiritual renewal, communal solidarity, and joyous festivities, marking the resurrection of Jesus Christ and the arrival of springtime in Greece.

REFERENCES

- Magiritsa: A Traditional Greek Easter Soup Recipe. (2022, April 13). Greek City Times. [https://greekcitytimes.com/2022/04/13/magiritsa-greek-easter-soup-recipe/]
- Greek Easter: Customs and Traditions. (2022, April 12). Greeka.com. [https://www.greeka.com/greece-culture/customs/easter/]
- Greek Easter Recipes. (n.d.). The Spruce Eats. [https://www.thespruceeats.com/greek-easter-recipes-1705284]

References to Similarities of Other Artifacts

Similarity of Greek Pithos Painted Surface Renderings to Phaistos Disc Spiral Design

Though the majority of scholars continue to point to the laborious task of painting common wears such as storage and transportation vessels for everyday use as "art" and "beliefs" of a civilization, no matter what continent it is from, the fact remains it is none of that. The artistic representation of patterns, such as spirals, comes from the singular design's appeal as a display, which allows the normal transfer by means of commerce as has always been the case. Simply put, a nice product sells. The actual usage of these symbols is for the recording of the date the product was either placed within the container, or when the product should be used by. Simple color dotting of specific location upon the spirals, for instance, quickly tells the owner/buyer of such information, much like today's labels and ink stamps on products. The Ancient Universal Language of the spiral for the calendar year and month maintains a global usage in these various vessels and provides a visually pleasing way to use the language while maintaining a transportable utilitarian means of listing a date.

The commonality of other types of ancient artifact usage similar to the Phaistos Disc design implementation further confirms the validity of the author's usage decipherment.

Background

The painted spirals on ancient Greek pithoi, large storage jars made of clay, were a common decorative motif that held symbolic and aesthetic significance. These spirals, often referred to as "meanders" or "key patterns," were intricately painted onto the surface of the pithos, enriching its visual appeal and reflecting the artistic conventions of ancient Greek pottery. Here's a description of the painted spirals on ancient Greek pithoi:

Geometric Patterns:

- The painted spirals on ancient Greek pithoi were part of a broader repertoire of geometric patterns used in Greek pottery decoration.

- These spirals often consisted of interconnected lines that formed continuous loops or coils, creating a visually dynamic and intricate design.

Thought Symbolism and Meaning:

- The spirals on ancient Greek pithoi were imbued with symbolic significance, although their precise meaning is subject to interpretation.

- Some scholars suggest that the spirals represented eternity, infinity, or the cyclical nature of life, reflecting the ancient Greek worldview and philosophical beliefs.

- Others propose that the spirals may have symbolized cosmic forces, natural phenomena, or spiritual concepts, aligning with the broader religious and mythological symbolism found in ancient Greek art.

Aesthetic Appeal:

- Beyond their symbolic meaning, the painted spirals on ancient Greek pithoi served an aesthetic function, enhancing the visual appeal of the vessels.

- The intricate patterns and rhythmic repetition of the spirals created a sense of harmony and balance in the overall design of the pithos.

- The use of contrasting colors, such as black spirals against a red or white background, added depth and dimension to the painted decoration, showcasing the skill and artistry of

- ancient Greek potters and painters.

Cultural Context:

- The painted spirals on ancient Greek pithoi were part of a broader artistic tradition that spanned centuries and influenced various aspects of Greek visual culture.

- Similar spiral motifs can be found in other forms of ancient Greek art, including pottery, metalwork, and architectural ornamentation, indicating their widespread popularity and cultural significance.

- The use of geometric patterns like spirals reflects the aesthetic preferences and artistic conventions of ancient Greek society, as well as the influence of mathematical and geometric principles in Greek art and design.

Archaeological Significance:

- The discovery of painted pithoi with spiral decoration in archaeological excavations provides valuable insights into ancient Greek pottery production, artistic techniques, and cultural symbolism.

- These artifacts contribute to our understanding of ancient Greek material culture and the role of pottery in everyday life, trade, and religious rituals.

- The preservation of painted pithoi in museum collections allows modern audiences to appreciate and study these ancient artifacts, preserving their cultural legacy for future generations.

- In summary, the painted spirals on ancient Greek pithoi were a distinctive decorative motif that combined symbolic meaning with aesthetic appeal. These spirals reflected the artistic sophistication, cultural symbolism, and technical skill of ancient Greek potters and painters, leaving a lasting legacy in the visual arts of ancient Greece.

REFERENCES:
- Boardman, John. "Athenian Black Figure Vases." Thames & Hudson, 1974.
- Neer, Richard. "Greek Art and Archaeology: A New History, c. 2500-c. 150 BCE." Thames & Hudson, 2012.
- Carpenter, Thomas H. "Art and Myth in Ancient Greece." Thames & Hudson, 1991.
- Osborne, Robin. "Greece in the Making, 1200-479 BC." Routledge, 2009.
- Woodford, Susan. "An Introduction to Greek Art: Sculpture and Vase Painting in the Archaic and Classical Periods." Cornell University Press, 2012.

References

1. Castleden, Rodney. "Minoans: Life in Bronze Age Crete." Routledge, 2002.

2. Branigan, Keith. "The Foundations of Palatial Crete: A Survey of Crete in the Early Bronze Age." Routledge, 2013.

3. Davaras, Costis. "Crete: Culture and Civilization." Ekdotike Athenon, 2004. https://commons.wikimedia.org/w/index.php?curid=3111462

4. "The Phaistos Disk" by Harriet Blitzer, American Journal of Archaeology, Vol. 96, No. 3 (July 1992), pp. 543-544.

5. "The Phaistos Disk: A New Way of Approaching a Famous Enigma" by Gareth Owens, Journal of Mediterranean Archaeology, Vol. 20, No. 1 (2007), pp. 135-139.

6. Title: "The Origins of Printing in China" Author: Tsien Tsuen-Hsuin Publication: The British Library, 1985 ISBN: 978-0712301356

7. Van de Mieroop, Marc. "A History of the Ancient Near East, ca. 3000-323 BC." Blackwell Publishing, 2007.

8. Cartledge, Paul. "The Greeks: A Portrait of Self and Others." Oxford University Press, 2002.

9. Beard, Mary, et al. "The Oxford Classical Dictionary." Oxford University Press, 2012.

10. Parpola, Simo. "The Helsinki Atlas of the Near East in the Neo-Assyrian Period." Helsinki University Press, 2001.

11. Parker, Robert. "Miasma: Pollution and Purification in Early Greek Religion." Oxford University Press, 1996.

12. Scarre, Chris, et al. "The Human Past: World Prehistory and the Development of Human Societies." Thames & Hudson, 2018.

13. Parker, Robert. "Miasma: Pollution and Purification in Early Greek Religion." Oxford University Press, 1996.

14. Rutherford, Ian. "Athenian Religion: A History." Oxford University Press, 2000.

15. Wycherley, R. E. "The Athenian Calendar." Harvard Studies in Classical Philology, Vol. 74 (1970), pp. 159-183.

16. Young, Rodney S. "The Athenian Festivals: A Commentary." Oxford University Press, 2010.

17. Beard, M., North, J., & Price, S. (1998). "Religions of Rome: Volume 1, A History." Cambridge University Press.

18. Forsythe, G. (2005). "A Critical History of Early Rome: From Prehistory to the First Punic War." University of California Press.

19. Ogilvie, R. M. (1986). "The Romans and Their Gods in the Age of Augustus." Routledge. https://en.wikipedia.org/wiki/Phaistos_Disc

20. Cavanagh, William, et al. "Mochlos IIA: Period IV: The Mycenaean Settlement and Cemetery: The Pottery." INSTAP Academic Press, 2013.

21. Castleden, Rodney. "Minoans: Life in Bronze Age Crete." Routledge, 2002.

22. Schoep, Ilse. "Mochlos IA: Period III: Neopalatial Settlement on the Coast: The Artisans' Quarter and the Farmhouse at Chalinomouri." INSTAP Academic Press, 2005.

23. Tzedakis, Yannis. "An Archaeology of Late Antique Pilgrim Flasks." British Archaeological Reports, 2003.

24. Wilkinson, Richard H. "The Complete Gods and Goddesses of Ancient Egypt." Thames & Hudson, 2003.

25. Boardman, John. "The Greeks: A Portrait of Self and Others." Oxford University Press, 2002.

26. Beard, Mary, et al. "The Oxford Classical Dictionary." Oxford University Press, 2012.

27. Burkert, Walter. "Greek Religion: Archaic and Classical." Harvard University Press, 1985.

28. Parker, Robert. "Miasma: Pollution and Purification in Early Greek Religion." Oxford University Press, 1996.

29. Woolley, Leonard. "Religious Life in Ancient Mesopotamia." Clarendon Press, 2011.Top of Form

30. Kondratiev, Alexei. "The Apple Branch: A Path to Celtic Ritual." Citadel Press, 2003.

31. McColman, Carl. "Celebrating the Seasonal Holy Days: A Collection of Seasonal Holy Day Celebrations." New Page Books, 2011.

32. Nichols, Ross. "The Book of Druidry." Thorsons, 1990.

   - Wilkinson, Richard H. "The Complete Gods and Goddesses of Ancient Egypt." Thames & Hudson, 2003.

   - Black, Jeremy, and Anthony Green. "Gods, Demons, and Symbols of Ancient Mesopotamia: An Illustrated Dictionary." University of Texas Press, 1992.

   - Green, Miranda. "Animals in Celtic Life and Myth." Routledge, 1992.

33. Papanastasiou, Ioannis, et al. "Beekeeping in Crete." Bee World, vol. 86, no. 4, 2005, pp. 95-102.

34. Sgardelis, Stefanos P., et al. "The Role of Honeybees (Apis mellifera L.) in Pollination and Conservation of Mediterranean Ecosystems: A Review." Journal of Apicultural Research, vol. 53, no. 4, 2014, pp. 425-437.

35. Block, Barbara A., et al. "Tracking apex marine predator movements in a dynamic ocean." Nature 475.7354 (2011): 86-90.

36. Karachle, Paraskevi K., et al. "A review of bluefin tuna (Thunnus thynnus) aquaculture: a case study from the Mediterranean Sea." Reviews in Aquaculture 12.1 (2020): 256-277.

37. Karakulak, Saadet, and Okan Akyol. "Recent occurrence of the Atlantic bluefin tuna, Thunnus thynnus (Linnaeus, 1758), in Turkish waters of the eastern Mediterranean Sea." Journal of Applied Ichthyology 24.1 (2008): 113-115.

38. Burkert, Walter. "Greek Religion: Archaic and Classical." Harvard University Press, 1985.

39. Parker, Robert. "Miasma: Pollution and Purification in Early Greek Religion." Oxford University Press, 1996.

40. Burkert, Walter. "Homo Necans: The Anthropology of Ancient Greek Sacrificial Ritual and Myth." University of California Press, 1986.

41. Magiritsa: A Traditional Greek Easter Soup Recipe. (2022, April 13). Greek City Times. [https://greekcitytimes.com/2022/04/13/magiritsa-greek-easter-soup-recipe/]

42. Greek Easter: Customs and Traditions. (2022, April 12). Greeka.com. [https://www.greeka.com/greece-culture/customs/easter/]

43. Greek Easter Recipes. (n.d.). The Spruce Eats. [https://www.thespruceeats.com/greek-easter-recipes-1705284]

44. Boardman, John. "Athenian Black Figure Vases." Thames & Hudson, 1974.

45. Neer, Richard. "Greek Art and Archaeology: A New History, c. 2500-c. 150 BCE." Thames & Hudson, 2012.

46. Carpenter, Thomas H. "Art and Myth in Ancient Greece." Thames & Hudson, 1991.

47. Osborne, Robin. "Greece in the Making, 1200-479 BC." Routledge, 2009.

48. Woodford, Susan. "An Introduction to Greek Art: Sculpture and Vase Painting in the Archaic and Classical Periods." Cornell University Press, 2012.

END REPORT

Minoan Culture and Artifacts Associated with Their Sun God

January 2024 White Paper by
Chris Hegg
Independent Researcher
chrishegg@hotmail.com

The Minoan Civilization is largely an enigma, having just glimpses remain of their culture through frescos and artifacts that stitch together an incomplete puzzle of who they were and what beliefs they maintained. Answering questions such as: who was this empire, what technologies did they possess, and what were their beliefs would unlock critical understanding of the Minoans. Those questions are paramount within this report where several key and abundant representations appear to embody their religion within advanced technology like calendar creation. Minoans associate objects, celebrations, festivals, and other creations with this religion that is dedicated to their Sun God and more importantly the solar analemma, the apparent track of the Sun in a figure-eight pattern in the sky each year. The report will cover the top physical pieces of evidence from their culture which provide an almost unbelievable similarity to the analemma, proving the validity of the Phaistos Disc as a calendar and how it related to Minoan culture.

Minoan Culture and Artifacts Associated with their Sun God

Many evidentiary artifacts, images and temple decorations appeared to reinforce the Phaistos Disc Calendar decipherment report. These pieces of evidence were collected to create this report later on the topic. They could well have been attached to the original report but do merit their own discussion due to the importance of each, if they can be proven to be legitimate findings within.

Phaistos Disc Design and Creation

The disc design of the spiral is represented as a template associated with the ancient language the author studies on petroglyphs of much older age. This association allowed the analemma to be implemented as a template overlay and the decipherment of the disc made in reasonable time. Several important symbols exist in key locations to allow "clocking" of the spiraled symbol groups around the analemma figure eight format.

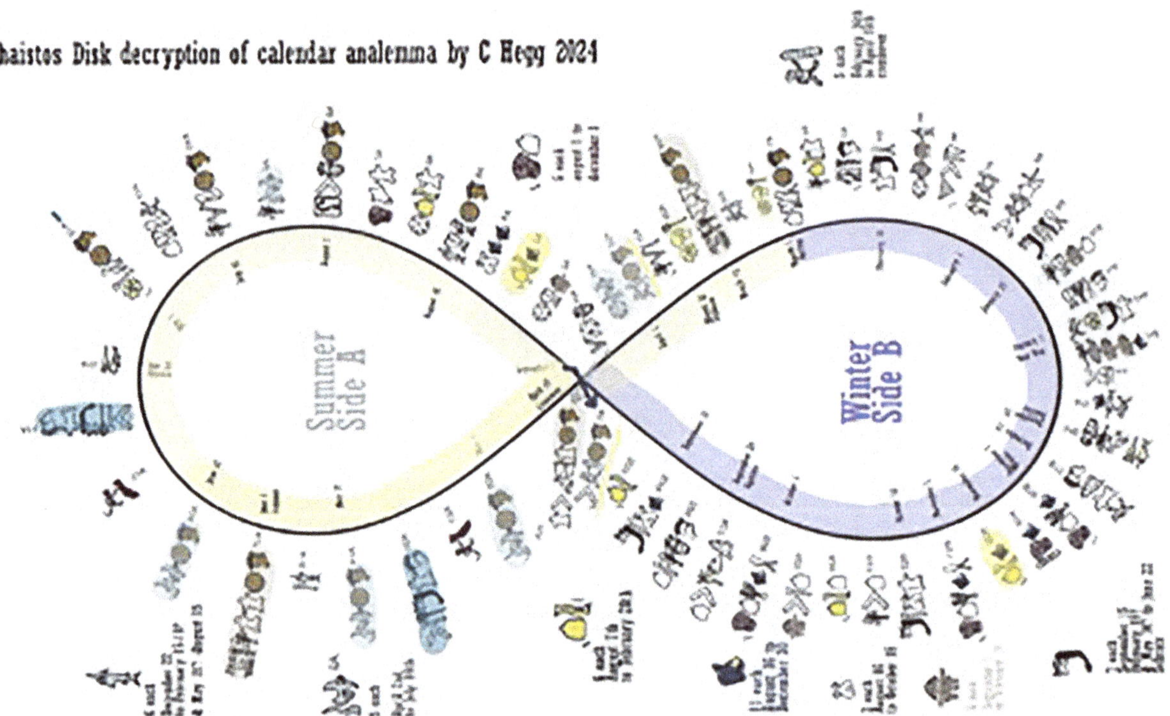

Image by author (Hegg C, 2024) of the Phaistos Disc Solar Calendar and it's use of the solar analemma as its template.

Solar Analemma

The Sun tracks around a pattern of the figure of eight and thus "rotates" in a counterclockwise and then clockwise direction to accomplish the complete journey around the figure. This rotation is simply designated with a placeholder in ancient language as a counterclockwise spiral and clockwise spiral depending on which hemisphere the Sun is positioned in during which months and seasons to depict the time or date of events. The proper visualization is reversed in the rotations as this ancient language projects the format using the Sun's shadow mark for reference as actual attempts to witness the true Sun's true trajectory in the open sky is impossible over time without much complication and fixed assets to align each day with to track movement. Simply projecting a shadow on the wall or ground allows easier defining of positions. Using such spiral configurations allows the observer to instantly know what is referenced is solar and not lunar, stars, or any other form of understanding. Such is also the case with the Phaistos Disc and Magliano Disc.

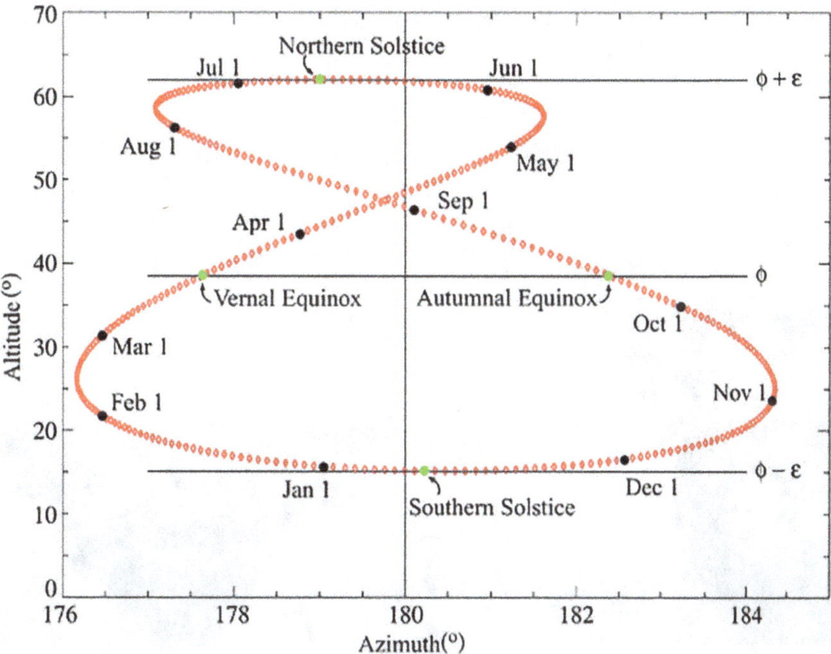

Image of public domain: solar analemma form. Note the figure eight direction of the Sun's apparent movement through the sky during the year.

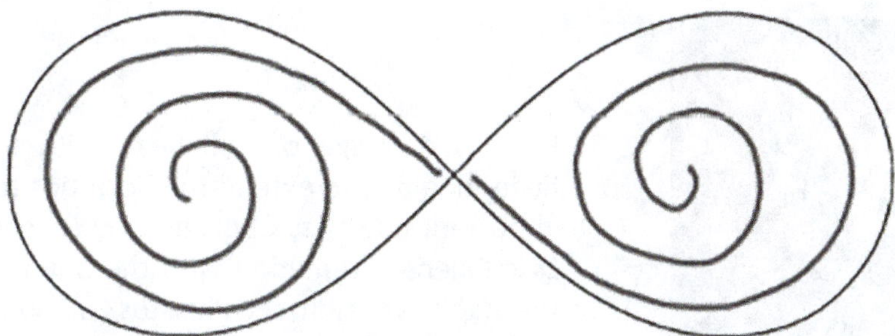

Spiral design by author: analemma "reversed spiral directions" of the sun's apparent movement rendered into a usable representation as a unified symbolic meaning of the ancient solar calendar. The Phaistos Disc goes a step further by refining the design to equal proportionate spirals within each hemisphere (and on each side of the artifact) moving in the same direction. This equally proportionate design is crucial to realizing substantial similarities and uses of other Minoan related artifacts and designations discussed further into the report.

Bull Head

The bull has a natural form that accentuates every aspect of its head with the solar analemma. The bull horn is an important symbol on the Phaistos Disc. The main similar characteristic is the wide curving horns that encompass the similar construction of the sideways analemma figure of eight. Each eye could represent the Sun God while it resides in the analemma's associated hemisphere as the bull's nostrils apparently do. Ears with openings may also indicate the analemma form as they again appear similar and had openings usable in the vessels. The detailing around the snout also signifies the analemma form and is accentuated with alabaster. Finally, the similar symbol to the double axe between the eyes on the forehead appears in a vertical position, possibly indicating the exact use of the axe in the worshiping as being the actual Solar God and its position anywhere within the analemma forever "splitting" the yearly formation. As the axe appears with goddesses only, it seems to more heavily indicate the splitting of the movement rather than the Sun God as the goddess manifests the analemma form and not the solar god.

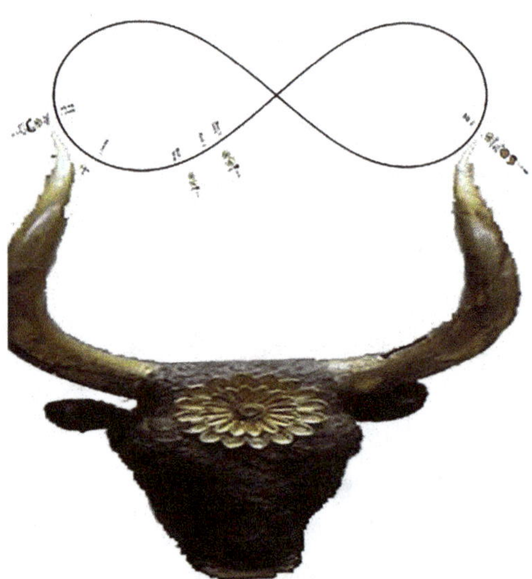

Image from Raddato, C. (2019, May 08). Bull's Head Rhyton from Knossos. *World History Encyclopedia*. Retrieved from https://www.worldhistory.org/image/10587/bulls-head-rhyton-from-knossos/ author inserted the form of the solar analemma above and between the horns.

Purchased image of bull head with flower symbol on head modified to extend the horn tips to contact the two important flower symbols equally spaced on the Phaistos Disc Calendar rendition with the bull head referenced to the author's deciphered Phaistos Calendar start date flower of March 1st. The axe symbol of the calendar was left to show reference within the horn tip symbols, completing the Minoan use of the bull as the Sun God.

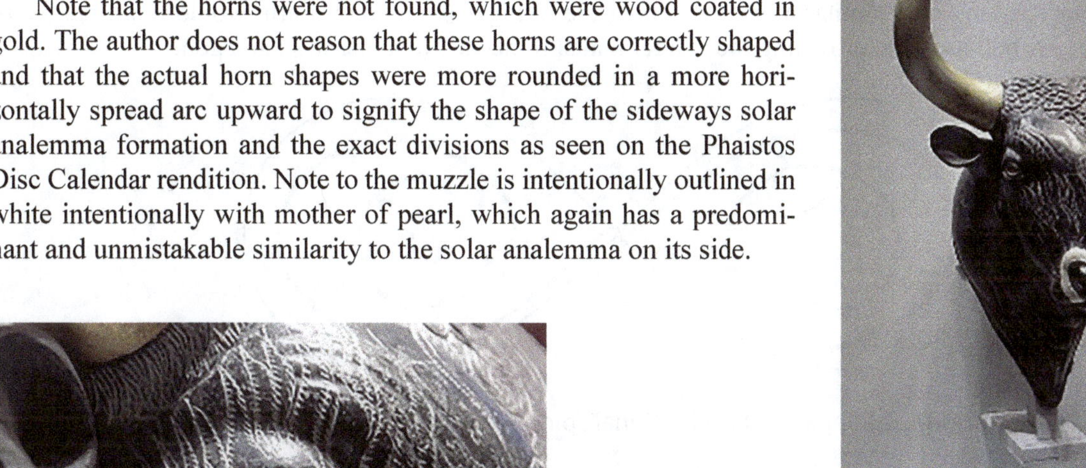

Bull's head shaped rhyton, from the palace at Knossos, c. 1550-1500 B.C.E. (Archaeological Museum of Heraklion, photo: Zde, CC BY-SA 4.0)

Note that the horns were not found, which were wood coated in gold. The author does not reason that these horns are correctly shaped and that the actual horn shapes were more rounded in a more horizontally spread arc upward to signify the shape of the sideways solar analemma formation and the exact divisions as seen on the Phaistos Disc Calendar rendition. Note to the muzzle is intentionally outlined in white intentionally with mother of pearl, which again has a predominant and unmistakable similarity to the solar analemma on its side.

Detail of bull's head rhyton from the palace at Knossos (Archaeological Museum of Heraklion, photo: Camille Gévaudan, CC BY-SA 4.0). Also note the markings around the eye referred to as "hair" engravings. Again, the author believes these markings depict solar flares designating the eye as the Sun God.

Raddato, C. (2019, May 08). Bull's Head Rhyton from Knossos. *World History Encyclopedia*. Retrieved from https://www.worldhistory.org/image/10587/bulls-head-rhyton-from-knossos/

Note in this closer image that when the bull is viewed from the front, there is a symbol that very closely resembles the design of the double-bladed axe in a vertical position directly between the eyes on the snout, further indicating the association of the analemma, axe, and other symbology relating to the Sun God. This symbol most certainly pertains to the solar analemma and is a very close match to the symbol of the Magliano Disc Calendar.

Bull Jumping

The act of bull jumping, specifically leaping over and through the horns of the bull, would further manifest a human form tumbling and twisting which mimics the solar rotational movement through the analemma figure of eight. Further enacting such similar movements over the living Solar God on Earth would reinforce the tie with their religious beliefs while providing the danger and skill needed to appease such a god.

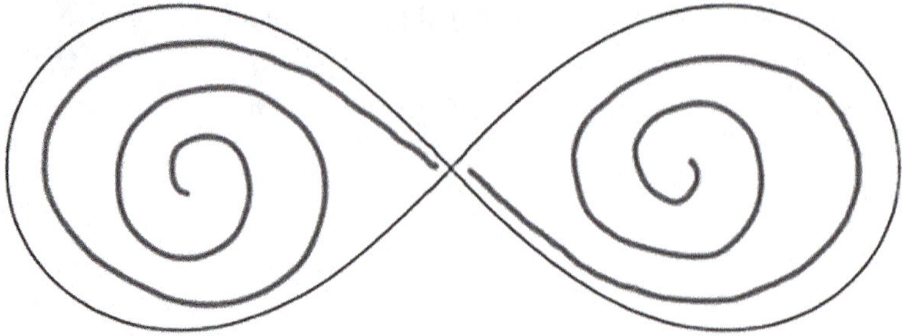

Author drawing of apparent bi-directional spiraling directions Sun of analemma.

Purchased image of a Minoan fresco depicting bull jumping.

Warrior Figure of Eight Shield Design

The easiest representation of the Solar God's movement along the solar analemma is the imagery of the warrior figure of eight shield design. It not only has the exact representation of the movement of their god but clearly overreaches in a large way implementing the entire shield design as their defending sprit of a religious deity. As with pretty much every single historic culture bearing the mark of their god onto the shield and even incorporated into the actual form of their spears and swords (such as the Catholic Cross) this one historic icon bears the most proof that the solar analemma and the Solar God were the main religious deity of the Minoans. This also adds to the growing proof the Phaistos Disc is a solar calendar by design.

The fact the shields bear covering of the bull hide is another connection to the worshiped bull and its relation to the Solar God. The final proof is the spiral designs on the walls along with the figure of eight shield and florets witnessed as key symbols on the Phaistos Disc further back the cumulative evidence the analemma and Sun were the most important object to the Minoans.

When compiled with bare breasted-women, snake goddesses, bull horns on the palace walls, frescos of bull leaping twirling movements of bravery, double-bladed axes and ring images, it is very compelling it all points to a combined objectification of the solar analemma, which in direct correlation is the solar movement in the sky and thus related to the Solar God, these all reinforce the Phaistos Disc as a solar calendar based off the template of the solar analemma.

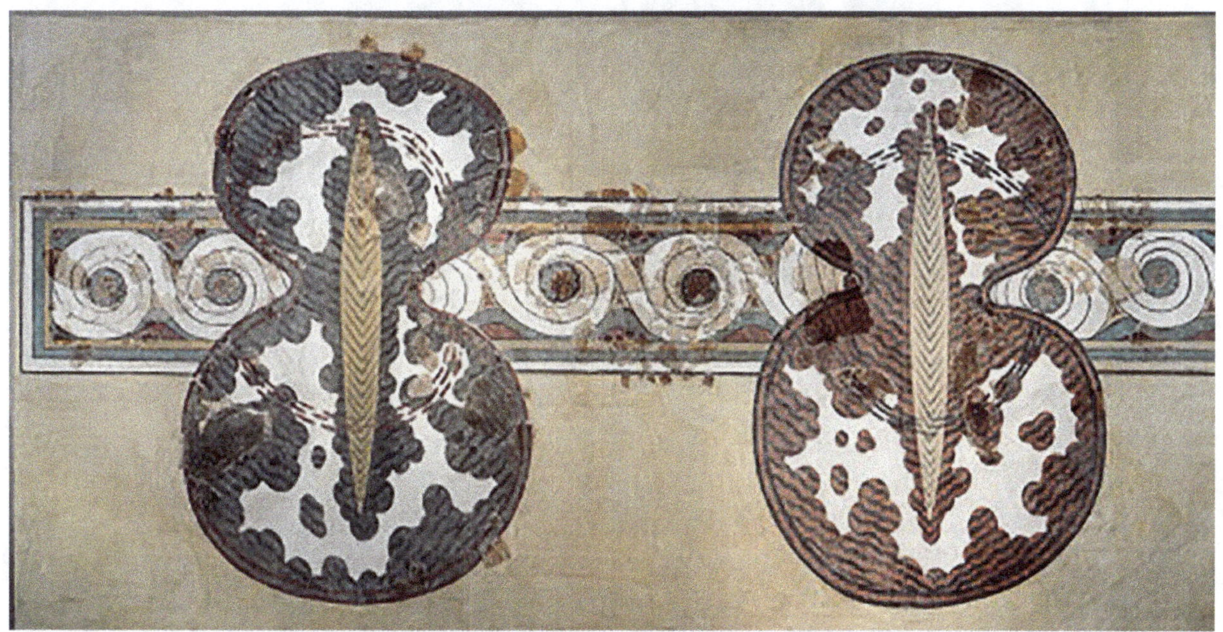

Image from public domain of shield representations right over the spirals and florets of the solar analemma.

Women's Apparel and Bare Breasts

The most relevant mirroring of the Minoan spiritual beliefs of the Solar God is the bare breasted women. The woman is also an important symbol on the Phaistos Disc Calendar. The breasts are the singular capable female part of the body which literally feeds the raised children of the society and thus their purpose and natural design mimicking the solar analemma in a living human form is unparalleled in comparison. When drawing the dual hemispheres of the analemma sideways one can clearly associate the two forms and so bare breasts were the manifestation of the Solar God's movements in the heavens on Earth and were to be worshiped. The fact the women used even lead oxide makeup to accentuate their lighter complexion also relates to mimicking the bright Solar God. The nipples may very much represent the Solar God within each of the analemma figure eight hemispheres and thus may have been accentuated as much as possible. The goddesses only wielding the double-bladed axe effigies may well relate the combined unity as a merged deity whereby the axe is the splitting of the analemma design and combined with the breasts represents the completed spiritual effigy and power.

Image from public domain: solar analemma representation of the breast. Note the Penistache pubic device of waist area possibly also representing a bull's reproductive parts and the raised outward angled hands similar to the grabbing of the solar analemma.

Double Bladed Axes of Crete

In Ancient Crete, the double axe only accompanied goddesses, never gods (*Schachermeyr, Fritz, 1964*) which again correlates both toward the symbolic movement of the analemma and not directly discussing any god, as it directly is the action of the Sun God worshiped. The double-bladed axe is a singular important symbol on the Phaistos Disc Calendar. The possibility then may be that the double head axe represents the actual Sun God, which always divides the solar analemma figure eight no matter where its position in the sky is. Being present with the goddesses could then suggest the bosom idolized as the manifestation of the solar analemma form is present always secondarily in nature to the axe (Sun God) and thus the two form the representation of the Sun God and its benevolent movement.

Image from Wikipedia contributors. (2024, April 15).

Image from public domain: several double-sided axes. Note that some edges at the tips have a projected curvature far beyond useful cutting distances and are of thin construction, indicating their sole purpose of worship and ceremonial use for the specific symbology of the analemma and its divisions. Massive axe heads exist with the same design function, as no other use for such large devices is known.

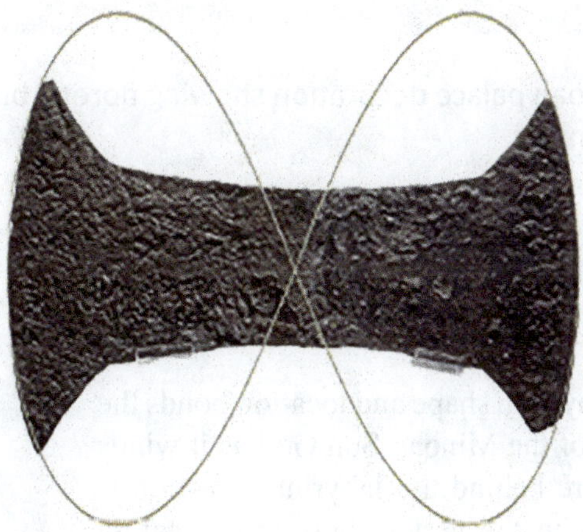

Purchased image: Minoan double-bladed axe overlaid with the solar analemma to signify the relation of the axe with the Sun God.

Building and Temple Architectural Designs

The palace decorations and architecture mimic the solar analemma in many aspects from the spiral decorations to the indicate maze of rooms below. The fact the bull horns are prominent upon the exterior walls suggests with no question it is solar related as well. These connections all point to the Solar God and the solar analemma as the highest worshiped divinity to the Minoans.

Image from public domain: Minoan palace decoration showing florets, but more importantly, interlacing spirals of the solar analemma.

Labyrinth

The very creation story of the labyrinth shape and location bonds the twisting and curvilinear movement of the Minoan Sun God as it winds around the solar analemma. The lore behind the labyrinth creation is that the living king's wife mated with the perfect bull, thus creating a half-man, half-bull child. This child must then be locked away with such a divine formation, which again shows the need to connect the king to the Solar God as a living manifestation of the two in the form of his child. Many labyrinth formations around the world depict ancient language focused around the solar movement, and this is no exception.

By originally-uploaded version by User:Blleininger, current version by AnonMoos - originally-uploaded version vectorized from File:Classical_7-Circuit_Labyrinth.jpg by JamesJen of labyrinth image found on a Minoan ring.

Pottery Designs

Spirals, figure eights and intricate rotational patterns are present everywhere on Minoan pottery. These designs are evidence of the focus on the solar analemma and the Solar God.

By Ijon - Own work, CC BY-SA 4.0, https://commons.wikimedia.org/w/index.php?curid=54970713. Many Minoan pottery designs designate the solar analemma movements similar to petroglyphs.

Snake Goddess

The snake goddess has identical representation of the solar analemma in her exposed breast outline and also holds onto the twisting and turning snake forms, which creatures mimic the very movement of the Sun God. The snakes also live underground but appear on the surface and must survive by basking in the Sun's rays, further solidifying them as the underworld creatures who work for the Solar God and thus their very form slithers and twists as representation of their god's divine movements.

Image from public domain: snake goddess again showing solar analemma formation of exposed breasts and holding winding, twisting snakes, another provocative representation of capturing the living solar worshipers of the underworld.

Signet Rings

Many ring images depict the same ritualistic and prized imagery of the double-bladed axe, bare breasts, shields and the Sun. It is worth mentioning these similar design elements talked about independently validate their cumulative representation within the coupled imagery of the rings, further giving proof the author's solar analemma connection is valid.

Image from public domain: Minoan signet ring. Note the Sun above, bare breasts, double-bladed axe and above them, the figure of eight shielded figure seeming to "paint" the whole scene or guard over them. All of the useful solar analemma designs and associated Sun present in one image except the bull as the Sun is present.

REFERENCES
- Hegg C, 2024, Report "The Phaistos Disk, the root design of the modern solar calendar, an early example of a bi-faced reproduction printing press template."
- Double Sided Axe only with goddesses and not gods. *Schachermeyr, Fritz (1964). Die minoische Kultur des alten Kreta [The Minoan Culture of Ancient Crete] (in German). Stuttgart, Germany: Kohlhammer. OCLC 325167. Abb. 85*
- Double sided axe Wikipedia contributors. (2024, April 15). Labrys. In *Wikipedia, The Free Encyclopedia*. Retrieved 01:19, April 19, 2024, from https://en.wikipedia.org/w/index.php?title=Labrys&oldid=1219076152

BULL HEAD:
- Hegg C, 2024, Report "The Phaistos Disk, the root design of the modern solar calendar, an early example of a bi-faced reproduction printing press template."
- Detailed bull's head rhyton from the palace at Knossos (Archaeological Museum of Heraklion, photo: Camille Gévaudan, CC BY-SA 4.0)
- Raddato, C. (2019, May 08). Bull's Head Rhyton from Knossos. *World History Encyclopedia.* Retrieved from https://www.worldhistory.org/image/10587/bulls-head-rhyton-from-knossos/

POTTERY:
- By Ijon - Own work, CC BY-SA 4.0, https://commons.wikimedia.org/w/index.php?curid=54970713

LABYRINTH:
- originally-uploaded version by User:Blleininger, current version by AnonMoos - originally-uploaded version vectorized from File:Classical_7-Circuit_Labyrinth.jpg by JamesJen

END REPORT

Decipherment of the Magliano Disc Solar Calendar, a Direct Link to the Modern Calendar

The Phaistos Disc Artifact as the root design of the modern solar calendar, an early example of a bi-faced reproduction printing press template.

January 2024 White Paper by
Chris Hegg
Independent Researcher
chrishegg@hotmail.com

Introduction

The Magliano Disc is a solar calendar with the spiral design rooted in the much older ancient language found in petroglyphs (2017 *Ancient Universal Language of Man*, C Hegg) which uses the spiral designation of the solar analemma, the figure 8 of the natural yearly Sun movement in the sky.

The Magliano Calendar Disc is a twenty-four-month solar calendar with a starting date on the Imbolc Holiday of February 1st. Side A runs from February 1st to September 1st, reasonably assumed as actually ending on September 2nd with verbiage of the crossover event, which is effectively the second crossover of the analemma. From the outer edge of Side B starting on September 3rd (the day of the second crossover event) and ending at the center on the month of January 15th, effectively ending on January 30th, the day before the Side A beginning.

The calendar disc is read from the beginning on Side A at the center, to the outside rim (left to right) where the calendar continues on the opposite Side B at the outside rim, where it continues along the spiral design to the center (right to left) where it ends. This pattern mimics the natural counterclockwise and then clockwise rotations of the Sun along its yearly path of the analemma.

The artifact, the author believes, was carved in a backward orientation of the letters in its entirety. This orientation is intended as a template for stamping onto a malleable surface, such as a wet clay or heated way, to create a forward-oriented calendar. When stamped together, it forms an entire analemma design that reveals the complete calendar.

The language could be argued to be read only right to left and the author has little interest in which way it reads and is beyond the scope of decipherment and this report. Either direction or orientation of single words or phrases has no bearing on each physical location within the calendar, but the author will show the designated symbols in the pre-determined reversed pattern in this report only. The author believes the actual proof of a mirrored orientation is present in the terrible designs of the letters themselves, appearing to be difficult to carve backward and thus resulted in very poor penmanship. This poor quality of the disc media, photos of the artifact, and the poor writing made the decipherment challenging. There are several very poor locations simply requiring a best guess unless the artifact is possibly seen directly.

As a note, some symbols reversed by the author while studying the object may be oriented incorrectly. It is important to clarify that this report prioritizes the use of letters and marks as placeholders in their designated locations on the calendar. Any errors of this type have no significant meaning in deciphering the physical layout and use of the device for this report, as they were not double-checked for proper direction. Sufficient similarities exist to easily compare the images to the artifact.

Side A and B Start and Ending Dates Defined

2024 Magliano Disk Calendar

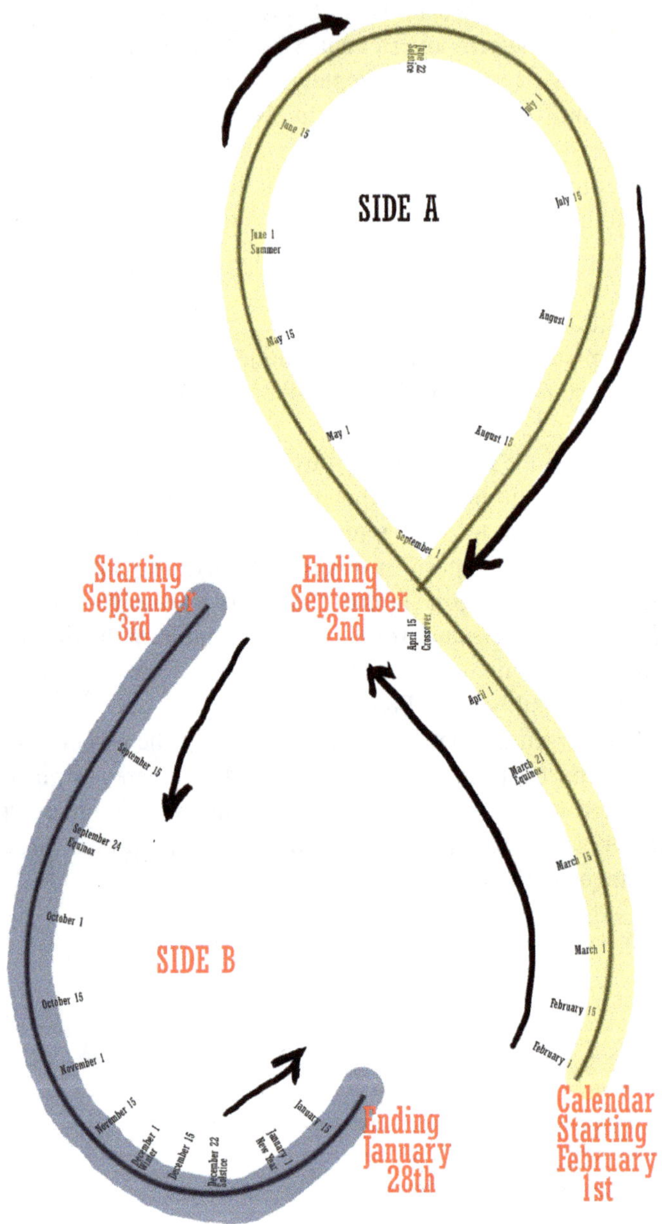

Image 1 by author: start and end dates of Side A and Side B in relation to the solar analemma. The noteworthy information is the starting on the Imbolc Holiday on February 1st and ending on the second crossover for Side A. Beginning at the second crossover and ending on January 31st ends the year. The disc is read from Side A center to outer edge and from Side B outer edge to its center.

Key Figure 8 Symbol in Relation to Clocked Positions Along the Solar Analemma

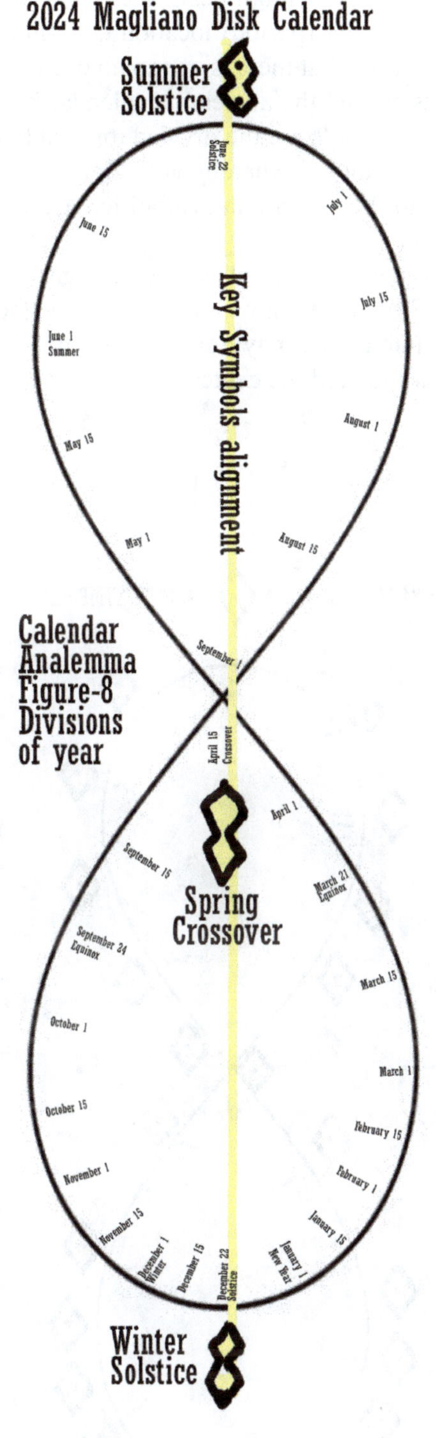

Figure 1

Image 2 drawing by author: analemma symbols in alignment positions dividing year in two. The symbols represent the figure 8 of the analemma.

Two symbols appear on Side A comprising of spring crossover and summer solstice. One symbol appears on Side B for winter solstice.

It should be noted the spring crossover symbol is incorporated into the April 15th month symbol group as that event corresponds exactly with that month's starting date.

Also worth noting is the summer solstice symbol designated with the one unusual month symbol within the same group. This correlates to a three dot (period) location denoting the highest, and therefore the most recognized location to place a month symbol, but there is no month during the June 22nd timeframe. This could denote how each month symbol exists around the analemma calendar by relating the meaning correctly with the analemma symbol 8 as all monthly symbols are the divided top and bottom hemispheres of the analemma. It could also be a position used as a leap-month whereby any adjustment period for days is defined after the summer solstice day. The connection to the analemma symbol letter group seems absolute, so there is some reasoning for the presence.

Also, very obvious on the disc for the summer solstice symbol group is the curvature of the spiral at that point "drops down" or "connects into" the outer rim spiral, which pays homage to the beginning of the solar physical decline in the sky toward autumn. One may note that on the Side B outer edge no such drop or jog exists along the spiral as it heads inward toward the center.

Month Symbols

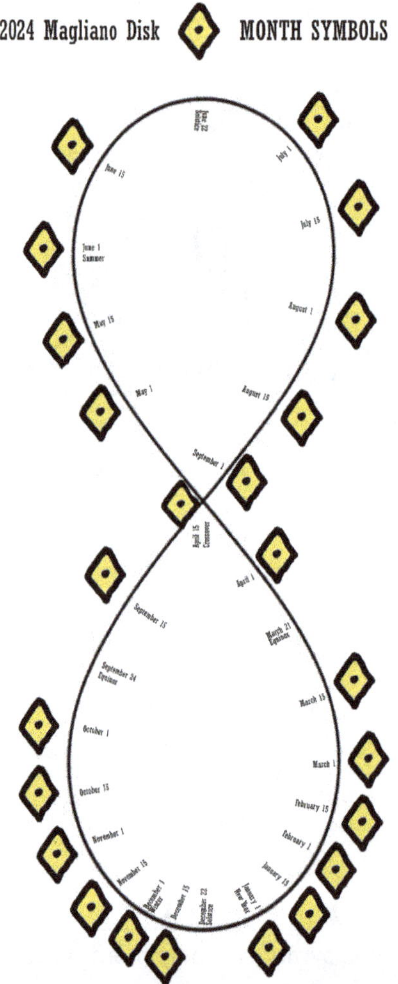

Fig 3 by author: representation of the month symbol of the individual broken hemispheres of the analemma symbol (8) and is thus a similar symbol. The period within denotes the "start" or "point" of the month. There are 24 months on the calendar. A central month symbol exists on both sides in the very center, denoting importance. Note the Side A "starting month" symbol does not have a period within it, denoting every month symbol after comprises of a "stopping point" period.

An unusual month symbol exists with the summer solstice group mentioned earlier. Used as a leap month, or to denote at the top of the analemma the breaking up of the figure 8 analemma symbol is unclear.

Another fascinating combination of month points exists in only two locations on the May 1st month and on the July 15th month. These groups comprise of the only double month symbol groups and bracket the summer solstice month symbol approx. 52 days prior and 23 days after. It may represent some other bracketing but their relationship to their specific symbol groups is absolute. These extra month symbols may also represent leap month locations.

Relevant Letter Groupings Between Some Months

Letter groups exist between months in locations of historic and modern importance such as Imbolc, Season starts, equinoxes, solstices, New Year (decidedly on this calendar as December 1st due to the carved line cutting across the spirals on the disc), and Rustica. Holidays and crossover events are all listed in the locations they should be. Devoid areas where such historically important events take place would be an impossibility when trying to design a calendar for any practical use. To note, however, between many months there are no listings of interest, showing this calendar is for the pure purpose of a calendar and not a device for another priority of interest that is listed along a calendar (such as a prayer wheel) and helped considerably in deciphering the positions due to the lack of other information. Also to note is that while the Side B symbol groupings show less months than the front, it is because of the vast amount of fill information listed that takes up the space, making the designer consider it more important to fill extra months with less fill required, onto Side A.

The deciphering process proved particularly challenging due to the artifact shading, dimples, and other visual issues apparent in the available photos of the device.

Month Symbol Groups

The following is a listing of the month symbol groups and the key analemma division symbol groups.

Month Symbol Groups

◊ΛΜΛ⌵·	February 1
Ɛ◊	February 15
ΛΛ◊	March 1
⋎⋁◊Ⅳ	March 15
⋁ᒧⲘ◊Ⲙ·	April 1
ᒧⅠΛLΛ◊	April 15
:ᒧⱤ◊ⅠΛL◊Ⅰ	May 1
Ѵ/Ⲙ◊Ⲙ	May 15
Ɣ⋁◊Ⅰ	June 1
ᒧⲘ⋁Λ◊	June 15
LΛᒧ◊	July 1
ᒧΛᒧ◊/Λᒧ◊	July 15
Ѵ/Ⲙ◊⋃·	August 1
/⋁◊/⋁	August 15
ᒧΛ⋃◊Λᒧ·	September 1
ⲘⲚꓭ⋎◊Λꓭ	September 15
ᒧƐ◊Ɣ⋁	October 1
◊Ⅰɣ𝖭Ɛᒧ	October 15
ⲘΔ◊Ⅰꓘⲅ·ᴇ	November 1
ƐƐⅠ·ⅠɣⅠ⋁ᗞΛᒧ	November 15
ꝂⲘƐⅠλⲘⅠ:	December 1
ⲘⲘ◊ᒧⲘƐL	December 15
Λ⋁ƐꝨ◊⋃⋋	January 1
𝖭Ⲙ◊ᒧꓢ	January 15

Dividing Symbols

Symbols	
Λ◊ᗞꓢ	Spring Crossover
ꝨΛLɣΛ◊:	Summer Solstice
ΛꝨ ᗞꓢⅠꓭΛᒧƐ	Winter Solstice

Image 4 by author: months and division analemma symbol groups.

The Magliano Disc Calendar Decipherment

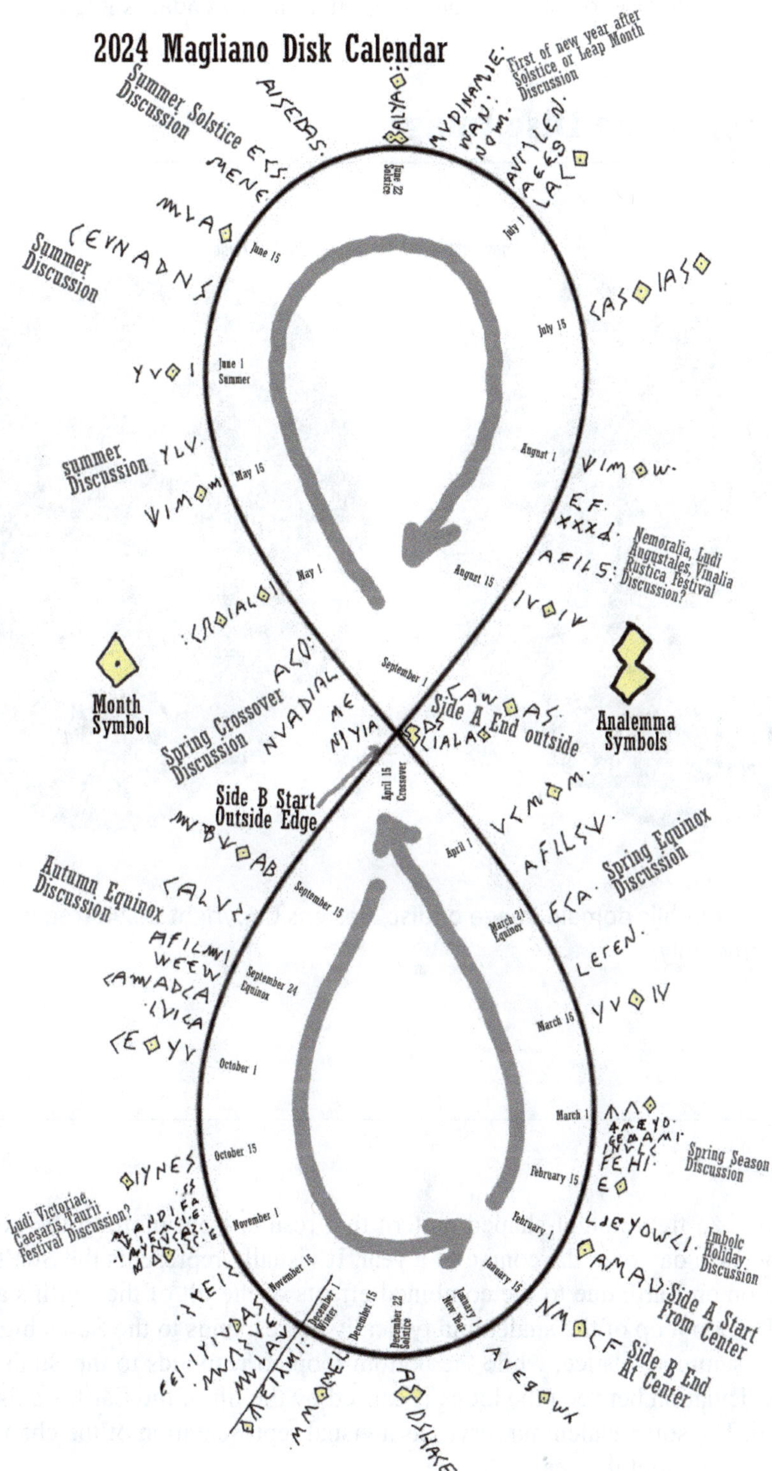

Image 5 by author: the Magliano Disc Calendar symbols along the solar analemma. Copyright 2024, for free use only with author's name and report name listed with it.

In comparison to the Phaistos Disc Decryption Report, this report is significantly easier. The author finds the letters unreadable, leaving little to discuss beyond this fact. The placement of two important symbols on the actual disc stands out as the most notable achievement by the designer. Apart from several periods consisting of two and three dots, there is little else to comment on except that this calendar is impeccably designed.

References of Months on Disc Image

Image 6 by author over public domain image of disc, designs Copyright 2024, free use with author name and report name only.

Background

Solar Analemma

The solar analemma is a figure-eight-shaped pattern that results from plotting the position of the Sun in the sky at the same time each day over the course of a year. It visually represents the Sun's apparent motion as seen from a fixed location on Earth due to the combined effects of the tilt of the Earth's axis and its elliptical orbit around the Sun. The top loop of the analemma typically corresponds to the Sun's highest point in the sky at solar noon during the summer solstice, while the bottom loop corresponds to the Sun's lowest point during the winter solstice. The deviation between the loops is caused by the tilt of the Earth's axis and the variation in the Earth's orbital speed. The solar analemma serves as a visual representation of the changing seasons and the Sun's changing altitude throughout the year.

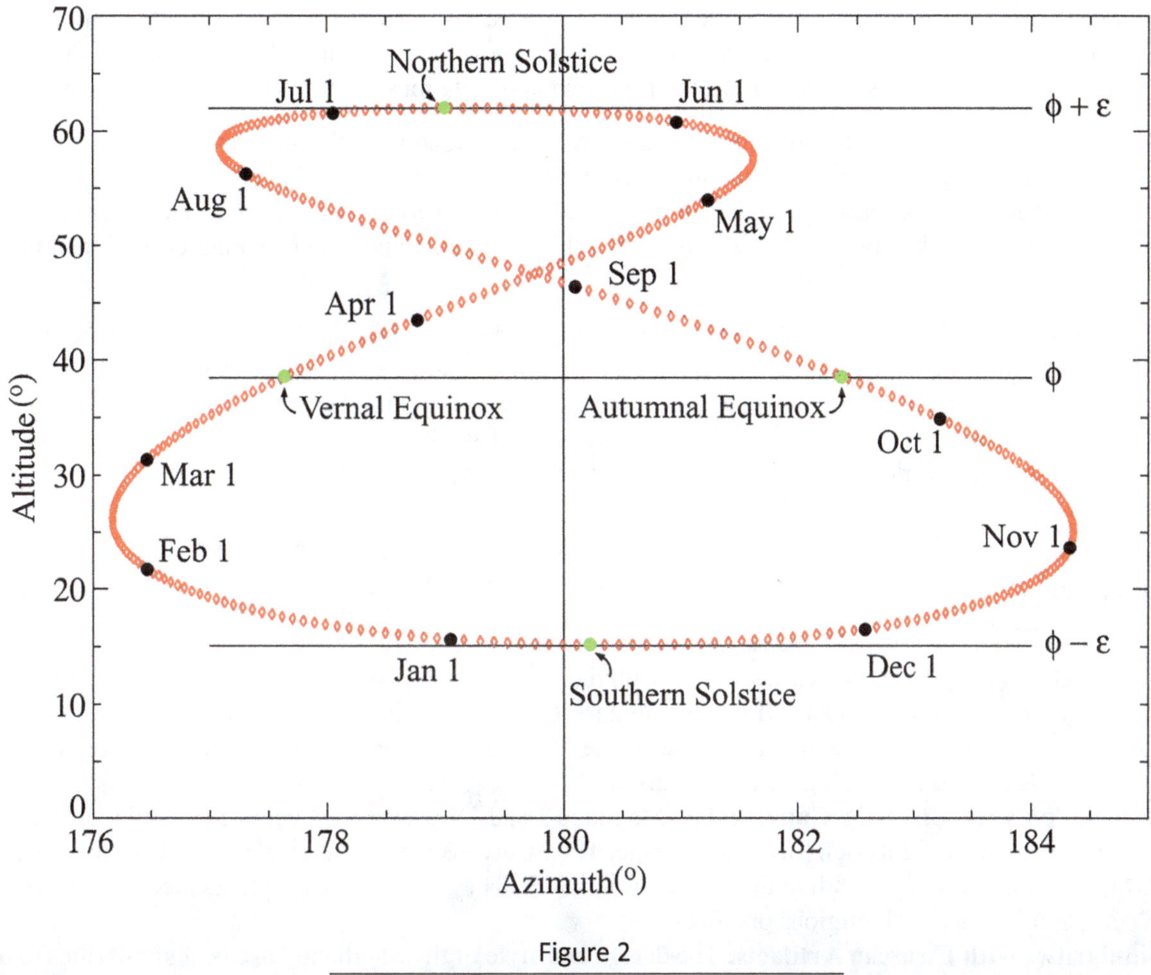

Figure 2

Image 8 from public domain: analemma Sun movement through the year. Note it moves reverse of the ancient language and author decipherment directions. This is because the ancient language uses the analemma as it is cast using a shadow onto a surface, which makes the representation backwards. No way is there a reliable means to observe the open sky while observing the actual Sun and be able to track or tell if the Sun moves and where, which is why the shadow is used. Imagine a stick between as it casts a shadow onto a wall, as the Sun moved left the shadow then moves right in mirror of the sunlight.

Magliano Disc

The Magliano Disc, also known as the Magliano Lead Disc or the Magliano Astronomical Disc, is an archaeological artifact discovered in Magliano, Italy in 1889. It is a small bronze disc, measuring about 15 centimeters (6 inches) in diameter, and dates back to the late 2nd millennium BCE, making it one of the oldest known representations of the sky and celestial bodies.

- **Background:** The Magliano Disc was discovered in a tomb in the Italian region of Tuscany near the town of Magliano. It was found alongside other grave goods, including pottery, weapons, and jewelry, typical of the Bronze Age burial customs in the region. The Magliano Disc is believed to have been buried with its owner, possibly as a symbol of status or a representation of their beliefs about the cosmos.

- **Description:** The Magliano Disc is made of bronze and features a series of concentric circles engraved on its surface. The circles are divided into sections, each containing a series of dots or indentations. Some scholars interpret these markings as representations of celestial bodies, such as the Sun, Moon, and stars, while others suggest they may represent constellations or other celestial phenomena.

- **Interpretation:** The exact meaning and purpose of the Magliano Disc remain a subject of debate among archaeologists and historians. Some interpretations suggest that it served as an astronomical instrument or calendar used for tracking the movements of celestial bodies or determining the passage of time. Others propose that it may have had symbolic or religious significance, representing cosmological beliefs or rituals related to the afterlife.

- **Significance:** Regardless of its precise function, the Magliano Disc is a valuable artifact that provides insights into the astronomical knowledge and cultural practices of Bronze Age societies in Italy. It demonstrates the importance of celestial observation and the symbolic significance of the sky in ancient belief systems. Studying artifacts like the Magliano Disc helps archaeologists and historians better understand the worldview and intellectual achievements of ancient civilizations.

Etruscan

The Magliano Lead Disc is often associated with the Etruscan civilization due to its discovery in the vicinity of Etruscan archaeological sites and its resemblance to other Etruscan artifacts. However, it's essential to note that the exact cultural context and purpose of the Magliano Disc within the Etruscan society remains a subject of debate among archaeologists and historians.

Association with Etruscan Culture: The Magliano Lead Disc was discovered in Magliano, Italy, near Tuscany, an area known for its rich Etruscan heritage. The Etruscans were an ancient civilization that flourished in central Italy from around the 8th to the 3rd centuries BCE. They developed a sophisticated culture with distinctive art, architecture, and religious practices.

Similarities with Etruscan Artifacts: The design and style of the Magliano Disc bear similarities to other Etruscan artifacts, such as bronze mirrors, votive offerings, and other religious objects. Its circular shape and engraved patterns suggest a possible connection to Etruscan cosmology, astronomy, or religious beliefs.

Similarities and Differences Between the Phaistos Disc and Magliano Disc
The Phaistos Disc, discovered on the island of Crete in the early 20th century, is an enigmatic artifact dating back to the Minoan civilization, which flourished during the Bronze Age. Like the Magliano Disc, it represents a fascinating archaeological puzzle, and there have been various theories proposed regarding its origin, purpose, and cultural significance. Let's explore some details for and against the association of the Phaistos Disc with the Magliano Disc:

For Association

1. **Geographical Proximity:** Both the Phaistos Disc and the Magliano Disc were discovered in the Mediterranean region, with the Phaistos Disc found on the island of Crete and the Magliano Disc found in the Italian region of Tuscany. The geographical proximity suggests potential cultural connections or interactions between the civilizations of these regions during the Bronze Age.

2. **Stylistic Similarities:** While the Phaistos Disc and the Magliano Disc are made of different materials (clay vs. lead) and have distinct designs, they share some stylistic similarities. Both artifacts feature circular shapes with engraved patterns arranged in a spiral or concentric circles. These similarities hint at possible cultural exchanges or shared artistic motifs between different ancient civilizations.

Against Association

1. **Cultural Context:** The Phaistos Disc is firmly associated with the Minoan civilization of ancient Crete, as it was discovered in the archaeological context of the Minoan palace at Phaistos. The Minoans had their own unique culture, language (Linear A script), and artistic traditions, distinct from those of other civilizations in the Mediterranean region.

2. **Material and Technique:** The Phaistos Disc is made of fired clay and features imprinted symbols arranged in a spiral pattern on both sides. The technique used to create the disc is characteristic of Minoan pottery and seals. In contrast, the Magliano Disc is made of lead and has engraved patterns on its surface, suggesting a different material and manufacturing technique.

Etruscan Language

The Etruscans were an ancient civilization that thrived in central Italy from around the 8th to the 3rd centuries BCE. While much about their language remains mysterious due to the limited surviving evidence, there have been some speculative theories regarding possible connections between the Etruscan language and Proto-Indo-European language, the hypothetical ancestor of the Indo-European language family, which includes English. However, it's important to note that these theories are highly speculative and have not been widely accepted by scholars. Here are some possibilities and considerations:

1. **Linguistic Similarities:**

   - Some linguists have proposed that the Etruscan language shares certain linguistic features with Indo-European languages, including English. These proposed similarities include phonological, morphological, and lexical elements.

   - For example, there have been comparisons drawn between Etruscan and Proto-Indo-European vocabulary, particularly in terms of basic lexical items such as kinship terms, numbers, and common nouns.

2. **Borrowings and Contacts:**

   - The Etruscans had significant interactions and cultural exchanges with neighboring civilizations, including the Greeks and the Romans. It's possible that they borrowed linguistic elements from these cultures, which could have indirectly influenced later languages, including English.

   - However, direct evidence of linguistic borrowings between Etruscan and Proto-Indo-European or its descendants is scarce and difficult to ascertain.

3. **Genetic Relationships:**

   - Some scholars have proposed that the Etruscan language may belong to a distinct language family unrelated to Indo-European. If this is the case, any similarities between Etruscan and Indo-European languages would likely be the result of linguistic borrowing or areal influences rather than genetic relationship.

4. **Lack of Evidence:**

   - One of the main challenges in studying the Etruscan language is the scarcity of surviving texts and inscriptions. Most surviving Etruscan texts are short and fragmentary, making it difficult to reconstruct the grammar and vocabulary of the language with certainty.

   - Without a more substantial corpus of texts or bilingual inscriptions, it is challenging to determine the extent of any linguistic connections between Etruscan and other ancient or modern languages, including English.

In conclusion, while there have been speculative theories regarding possible linguistic connections between the Etruscan language and Proto-Indo-European, including English, the evidence remains inconclusive. The study of the Etruscan language continues to be a subject of ongoing research and debate among linguists and historians.

References

Here are some general suggestions for finding references on the topics discussed within this report:

1. **Magliano Disc and Etruscan Civilization:**

   - Bonfante, L., & Bonfante, G. (2002). The Etruscan Language: An Introduction. Manchester University Press.

   - Pallottino, M. (1978). The Etruscans. Indiana University Press.

   - Haynes, S. (2000). Etruscan Civilization: A Cultural History. Getty Publications.

   - Barker, G. (1993). The Etruscans. Blackwell Publishers.

2. **Phaistos Disc and Minoan Civilization:**

   - Shelmerdine, C. W. (2008). The Cambridge Companion to the Aegean Bronze Age. Cambridge University Press.

   - Cline, E. H. (2014). The Oxford Handbook of the Bronze Age Aegean. Oxford University Press.

   - Castleden, R. (2002). The Knossos Labyrinth: A New View of the "Palace of Minos" at Knossos. Routledge.

   - Preziosi, D., & Hitchcock, L. A. (1999). Aegean Art and Architecture. Oxford University Press.

3. **Etruscan Language and Proto-Indo-European:**

   - Rix, H. (2008). Etruscan. In R. Woodard (Ed.), The Ancient Languages of Europe (pp. 141-165). Cambridge University Press.

   - de Simone, C. (2009). Etruscan. In R. D. Woodard (Ed.), The Cambridge Encyclopedia of the World's Ancient Languages (pp. 966-985). Cambridge University Press.

- Schumacher, S. (2013). Etruscan. In P. O. Müller, I. Rutherford, & S. Schumacher (Eds.), Etruscology. Walter de Gruyter.

- Wallace, R. W. (2008). The Etruscan Language. Manchester University Press.

4. **Magliano Disc and Solar Analemma:**

- Magliano Disc: Unfortunately, specific references on the Magliano Disc may be limited, as it is a relatively lesser-known archaeological artifact. You may find information in academic journals, archaeological reports, or books on Etruscan archaeology.

- Solar Analemma: Meeus, J. (1997). Mathematical Astronomy Morsels. Willmann-Bell.

- Morrison, L. V., & Stephenson, F. R. (2004). Historical Values of the Earth's Clock Error ΔT and the Calculation of Eclipses. Journal for the History of Astronomy, 35(1), 327-336.

- Seidelmann, P. K. (Ed.). (1992). Explanatory Supplement to the Astronomical Almanac. University Science Books.

- "Analemma" in Encyclopedia Britannica.

- Di Sconosciuto - Baden State Museum Karlsruhe: The Etruscans. Karl Theiss Verlag, Stuttgart C.E.2017, page. 295., Pubblico dominio, https://commons.wikimedia.org/w/index.php?curid=83631331

END REPORT

Background of Ancient Universal Language as the Root of the Artifact Creation

Babel

I will attempt to show what existed before this "information darkness" when a Universal Language was made and taught to all the people of every land so such things as global trading and peace could be accomplished. This was not an esoteric code. It was meant to be globally learned. The Hebrew Bible describes this Universal Language existing later at Babel as they tried to make a "tower" to the heavens and the language was ultimately changed to seven individual languages. The separate groups were divided for this effort and spread to the corners of the globe to be forever lost. The Universal Language was used before this by cultures to build magnificent monoliths of understanding for the universal clock on every continent in a global setting not seen since, well, after Babel, (the legendary homeland where the tower to heaven was being built and stopped by God: Gen. 11:4–9). I believe that the ancient history of all these monumental undertakings everywhere, to "reach" to the heavens, survived as the story in the bible.

This combined effort to make a global capacity of understanding of the heavens that would last eternity, was thwarted sometime between then and now. The result is the loss of the old world's efforts and above all the loss of our global connection of peace, by means of the Universal Language, which in turn allowed for trade and expanding ideas from the global community. Peace was evident by the thousands of mega-projects developed by independent societies from every corner of the globe. The fact these ancient projects, when compared with the Universal Language, consistently use the same symbols—albeit rendered in monumental, earthly materials—suggests they were designed not just to endure over time but to withstand unknown calamities that could otherwise, and did, destroy all other human creations of that era. The information embedded in the physical forms and designs of theses structures reveal a timeless aspiration: just as today, the greatest wish of all was for world peace. The enduring desire for harmony had been a constant throughout history. So to was it then, as it has always been. Today, however, this timeless wisdom is increasingly overshadowed by contemporary higher education systems that often suggest modern humans uniquely evolved to understand concepts like art, family, death, and invention. The fact is, ancient humans were just as intelligent, if not more so, in their ability to understand and master their natural environment. New explorations into the past gradually reveal a more accurate understanding of history. However, none of theses discoveries seem to prompt a return to old institutions to correct the misleading teachings or to apologize for the misconceptions perpetuated by outdated theories. I am stating here I can live in the environment with information contained in the petroglyph language I proclaim to understand in this book. At the same time, I assert that most archaeological papers on petroglyphs offer little to no valuable information. In my view, the insights in these papers are often less credible than the petroglyphs themselves, with some scholarly interpretations seeming more influenced by speculative or disjointed theories than by historical accuracy.

Ancients

The Ancients taught the Universal Language. There are sites dedicated as classrooms, but I suspect most childhood teaching was done on panels with chalk and charcoal and dirt drawings as they went, and is lost to us. Some historical records of ideogrammic writing can be found among families and tribes that traveled across the globe and throughout America.

Who were these distant people? I can only answer as the "Ancients," a group of races, like today, that managed their own territories. From mummified remains it is known there were dark headed Caucasians in the West as well as giants with red hair. Indigenous legends describe a variety of people, including small beings, Caucasian individuals of regular size, and others who lived just thousands of years ago. Even Meriwether Lewis documented tribes with lighter skin and round eyes during his expedition. Such writings against this new land we call America may have even led to his demise. The territories of all of these lands around the globe make it absolute that territories had to be split up to keep proper control of the regions. Thus, empires were established, and their influence extended through various regions, a pattern observed throughout modern history when empires expand beyond their borders. Although wars erupted, it is evident that every society capable of doing so constructed enduring monuments designed to withstand the ravages of time and conflict. These grand structures reflect humanity's unified and unparalleled effort to preserve and convey knowledge to future generations. Again when I ponder why, I am struck with the sheer inhuman efforts it took and ask why. Why is this information needed for us in the future? Why did they realize we needed to know this information? If this was the case, it was evidently understood that 1) the effort was necessary, 2) it was inevitable, and 3) it was imperative for everyone to contribute to constructing monumental and impressive structures. These sites were designated to be so significant that future generations could not easily dismiss them, addressing the human tendency to overlook what seems unimportant or incomprehensible, such as petroglyphs. The builders likely believed that their efforts would make a lasting impact and be remembered through the ages. More importantly, they were convinced that their work would eventually be understood in time to address any critical issues before it was too late. I am speculating about the reasons behind the numerous megaliths around the world that share similarities and consistently convey the same information through the Universal Language. There must be a significant and profound reason for this widespread similarity, given the consistency of these massive structures across various locations and eras. I find it hard to identify specific, absolute events that are certain to recur. It is even more difficult to determine which of these events would necessitate the construction of monumental structures on a global scale thousands of years ago. Could a rogue planet rotation like the fabled Planet X be coming back around again that we need to know about? Could the reality of severe global warming be cyclic and have catastrophic consequences to the world, so bad a future warning was needed to be sent to prepare? Could it be that ancient structures were built to warn of recurring cosmic events, such as a return to a darkened region of space every few thousand years, as some ancient stories suggest? Or perhaps they were meant to signal cyclical magnetic pole reversals or catastrophic solar flares? Other potential calamities seem insufficient to explain why entire populations would dedicate such immense effort to create monuments as warnings for future generations.

I have a theory as to why the great Universal Language you will see in this book vanished when looking at the Bible's stories and today's evidence of these locations and people. The Bible tells of the uselessness and ego of man to build such a massive stairway to heaven in the Tower of Babel, The Old Testament, Genesis I. It appears that every culture made monoliths and cities and dedicated much to build and leave behind the great showings of their cultures' individuality and abilities. The Greeks, Romans, Polynesians, Aztecs, Mayans, Sumerians, Egyptians all demonstrate remarkable brilliance. Their understanding of life's cycles and their language inspired them to showcase their greatness through these monumental stone creations, aiming to match or surpass the achievements of their contemporaries.

This over-usage of manpower and the land's resources led to ignoring other basic needs and harmony with the Earth. On Easter Island for instance, nearly all the trees were completely depleted, and the local tribe was nearly extinct by the time modern explorers arrived. They used up the resources constructing the megalith statues surrounding the island. The Inca's appeared to have destroyed their entire jungle environment making oven baked brick for construction of their cities and temples, leading to the abandonment of their empire's ways. In every aspect, they gradually undermined their own survival in their quest to create these monumental structures. The resources committed to the build deforested whole regions and devastated food resources, eventually coming full circle to destroy the very empire everyone backed to build such accomplishments.

Among many, the Polynesians, Myans, Aztec and Egyptians experienced widespread devastation of their lands. This destruction was often attributed to erosion and other natural imbalances resulting from resource depletion caused by extensive monument-building activities, such as deforestation. These building projects were then considered poorly, and man was punished for his commitment to such feats and the legends survived the times. Man mostly buried or destroyed these amazing accomplishments or simply walked away.

In most instances the empire vanished as people walked away from it or destroyed it. Just as it happened in the past, it is likely to happen again, as human behavior often follows predictable patterns in group dynamics. Where culture becomes fixed, men in power become unyielding and there is no way out as a nation but to go along with it in unit until the end is met and the group is no longer able to maintain those fixed ways.

Ancient societies killed for sacrifice, got conquered by technologically superior neighbors or died under geologic calamities like Pompei. Modern societies are closely intertwined economically and religiously, as clearly demonstrated by the patterns seen in every world war and conflict. So as it is today, it was in the past, and so economics of trade and religious differences spurred similar unrecorded wars. The melting of the ice sheets and the resulting massive water runoff from the last ice age led to the loss of ancient knowledge about the Universal Language and the purpose behind the monuments. As the ice and waters receded, the super highways that connected us all vanish. Where man once floated to each other in ease, the lakes and byways dried up and man had to walk. These distances of dry land finally ended such connections and the great rebirth of man began as the old knowledge slowly died away.

The Walker Lake Paiute Tribe told Fremont, meeting him in his 1846 expedition, that the Ute tribes got over 300 warriors together from all over the Nevada western area to end the giants who were rumored to eat them once and for all due to their constant harassment of the Utes. They caught thirteen of the giants near the lake and drove the giant red heads back to the cave over 100 miles away where they burned brush in the opening to kill them after they would not surrender. They called them the Se-Ti-Cah which meant "Tully eaters" (an extinct type of stalk resembling a cat tail) because they ate Tully and actually were said to live on Tully raft cities on Pyramid Lake! The red hair of one giant was woven into the Chief's Princess' dress. The Paiutes, like most I've read about, they told Fremont that they did not create the petroglyphs, which had existed long before their arrival, 1,500 years ago. They suspected that the giants were the ones who made them. They recounted capturing a giant and torturing him to death in an attempt to decipher the meaning of the petroglyphs, but the giant died without revealing anything. They believe that if the petroglyphs could be ever read, it would bring peace to Earth. According to the Utes, all tribes once spoke the same language and could easily visit each other by water. However, as the waters dried up, travel became difficult, leading to the tribes' separation, changes in their languages, and the replacement of brotherhood with conflict.

ABSTRACT

On the west side of the Winnemucca Lake subbasin, Nevada, distinctive deeply carved meter-scale petroglyphs are closely spaced, forming panels on boulder-sized surfaces of a partially collapsed tufa mound. The large, complex motifs at this side are formed by deeply carved lines and cupules. A carbonate crust deposited between 10,200 and 9,800 calibrated years B.P. (ka) coats petroglyphs at the base of the mound between elevations of 1202 and 1206 m. Petroglyphs above the carbonate crust are carved into a branching form of carbonate that dates to 14.8 ka. Radiocarbon dates on a multiple-layered algal tufa on the east side of the basin, which formed at an elevation of 1205 m, as well as a sediment-core-based total inorganic carbon record for the period 17.0–9.5 ka indicate that water level in the Winnemucca Lake subbasin was constrained by spill over the Emerson Pass Sill (1207 m) for most of the time between 12.9 ± 0.3 and ≥ 9.2 ka. These and other data indicate that the lake in the Winnemucca Lake subbasin fell beneath its spill point between 14.8 and 13.2 ka and also between 11.3 and 10.5 ka (or between 11.5 and 11.1 ka), exposing the base of the collapsed tufa mound to petroglyph carving. The tufa-based 14C record supports decreased lake levels between 14.8–13.2 ka and 11.3–10.5 ka. Native American artifacts found in the Lahontan Basin date to the latter time interval. This does not rule out the possibility that petroglyph carving occurred between 14.8 and 13.2 ka when Pyramid Lake was relatively shallow and Winnemucca Lake had desiccated.

My Strengths of Decipherment

My strengths of decipherment began around 13 years of age. Years after I saw my first petroglyph shown to us by an old Paiute Indian woman. I recall a very dusty and miserably hot sunny day when we drove out in an old faded yellow Apache pickup my Grandpa bought from the Forest Service. The truck had no air conditioning and as a kid I got carsick easy, but refused to ever be left behind! The dirt road seemingly went on forever as it led into the deepest of the valleys where no human lived within 25 miles. I remember how amazed I was at the size of the world and I was old enough to start remembering locations, and this was the furthest I remembered traveling to. The old woman was scary to me, talking real light, but with a very raspy voice with a smile with few teeth. Being Piute, she was heavy set and short, long hair down her face and she had a "snake stick" she said. I knew she must have been a witch and could turn the stick into a snake at a whim I took that as! I had to sit with her in the bed of the truck when we picked her up for "company" and I knew I would not finish this journey alive. She ignored me as we bounced along the desert to a point the road gave out to a wash to deep to cross and we had to walk. My now dusty laden sweat being in the sun was compounded by loosing my hat along the way and I dare not stop my Grampa to retrieve it. Later the kind woman somehow recovered my hat and got it back to us later, for the moment however she remained scary. I knew it was a long day, because this woman looked 90 and with her snake stick, it was going to be a slow trip, but I was wrong again! I remember she had sheep in the valley and lived in a very shanty house built into the side of the hill half buried in the rock. She proved immediately too much for my teen legs and in no time we were all soon trailing far behind her in her seeming dash up the valley! We never caught up to her until she stopped at the first panel rock of a man appearing to flail his arms and legs with fingers open. That scared me less than her apparent lack of any hard breathing and excitement explaining this was the start of the site. Over two miles of grueling uphill races pursued chasing her to each new site. I lost interest in the central sites just worrying about surviving this trip and keeping my portrayed tough appearance intact. I remember one shocking rock with writing that she said water ran over the symbols when it rained, but that was it. She wore a cape of sorts, like a large dingy shawl covering her body which apparently shaded and kept her cool, as I remember no sweat from her through my salt burned eyes. I was uninterested until we came to the upper large panel site! Here was our last rock to visit. She called it the "Dead King Rock", matching her words to a image of a large upside down male body with no head and many amazing symbols surrounding the entire rock. She said the giants buried their king and this is the story. I was hooked for life the second I laid eyes on this rock! She captivated my curiosity with legends of giant red headed whites here from long ago they called the Ancient Se-Ti-Ca and the fact that they wrote the symbols, not the Indians! She told us that a small group of 3 were encountered by her (this story could have been referring to a story from her mother, I could not understand her completely?) while they were traveling not far from here heading back toward Walker Lake direction, leaving the mountain pass just a half mile behind them. They spotted 3 giants walking toward the very gap they exited on their way into this area and everyone got excited and dropped everyone to the ground behind brush as they watched the giants move to their left about 1 mile away. She asked her mom why they were so worried about the 3? Because in their group of women and children there were mostly armed warriors and the group totaled 13! The mother told her they would have no chance if they were spotted and they would have to flee if the giants turned! She told her "look at them, they are to be given as much room as you can give them, they are vicious and will eat you!" They waited crouched and hidden until well after the giants entered the canyon and disappeared and their immense height was visible even from that distance, carrying noticeably long spears. Then she was terrified forever of them and never seen one again.

Background

I had a United States Air Force job doing the old school Morse Code and learned fundamentals in cryptology. Since morse code is a very low power capable communications system, the signal sent can be heard by anyone listening to that frequency around the world. So the act of encrypting the message so it could not be read by an enemy was vital. The messages were sent by scrambling the language into what seemed to be gibberish. There wasn't a secret key used to break the sequence of numbers and letters to keep it confidential. The enemy is constantly attempting to crack that key, which led to the ongoing struggle of both sides continually adapting and changing the code and keys. This is what is known as cryptology. Cryptology was used probably since the beginning of the first hiding spot used by man!

Universal Language Symbols

UL symbology is based off of concepts. Two categories are incorporated in these concepts, sign language and nature. The nature concept combining both environmental foundations and animal actions. Nature and sign language can be mimicked with drawn symbols representing the movements of sign and nature when there is movement, but can also depict inanimate object forms and styling!

Sign

Hand motions match the one language hands can gesture- sign language! Many books exist on sign, but it is mostly white man sign we know today. Sites referenced the fact that white sign users could communicate with Native Indians and that the sign language of both only differed slightly but was about 80-85% compatible, *Mallery, Sign Language Among North American Indians Compared With that among other peoples and deaf-mutes first annual report of the bureau of ethnology to the 1881* is one of the first and best compilation of information. In reading hand motion science, there is much reference to the limitations of movements and similarities to natural gestures all humans do. A simple search of the most used gestures gained the path of the finger as the number one gesture, then the point (of the finger tip). *LaVan Martineau, The Rocks Begin To Speak*, was the first writer of sign language connections with petroglyphs and to comprehend the connection. My research and understanding of symbology on petroglyphs is a radical redirection from any before. I never intended to write a book on the topic and keep the information secret, then I started teaching my children and the realization of the need for this information became clear. Without understanding of the most important symbols most prolific in the world, I could not do it. As the decades progressed, I connected much more man made objects to this language and now it has progressed to my backyard to the globe!

Modern Images

In today's world there are many aspects of our lives quickly switching back to ideogrammatic. The Visual language uses images due to the vast language barriers the world now faces! Why? It is Because we have become a more mobile society able to migrate easier to foreign lands and co-exist with trade, just like in the ancient past. I know English modern language and that is it! I would be lost elsewhere if it wasn't for the street signs having black outline images of people crossing roads with legs open in a "walking" position my brain instantly recognizes, or my rental car dash lights all made of basic images like blinker arrows, gas pump, seatbelt over a sitting body and so on! If you took that dashboard out of the car and delivered it to an Indian 300 years ago a gas pump would be unrecognizable. Or would it? A pump image has several connected parts on it! The Indian could show you the gas hose going from the blocky pump to the pump handle as a connected item and part of the pump probably assuming it was flexible due to its sharp and unnatural curvature. He could identify it was something on the ground and was an object, that if you had laying around he could point out from recognition! So even a pump symbol could have some decipherment by a person due to some obvious hints.

He would immediately recognize the arrow symbol as used to point in a direction (like his projectile weapon's end where the arrow tip first came from). The arrow, thus broadhead tip of a projectiles end, has and is used by absolutely every culture in the world even to this day to point the way to something! It is interesting the obviousness of any direction symbol being symmetrically shortening toward the point of travel specified, being exactly like the penetrating end, which is required of any weapons delivery tip for penetration. That obviousness of similarity is ignored as a petroglyph symbol, yet be acceptable as a war symbol in other world languages like the Egyptian, Mayan and Encan. Because if just one symbol was accepted on petroglyphs, it would prove that petroglyphs are a language and thus not just independently drawn shaman drug art.

Here is a Mallery image from the book Sign Language Among North American Indians Compared With that among other peoples and deaf-mutes first annual report of the bureau of ethnology to the 1881. It is clear not only is he displaying the hand positions, but path lines in the form of dash paths. Closer observation shows the paths begin with the arrow point (or tail) < and the ending of the path is a circle with a dot in the center (a holding in place symbol). Then a final arrow point starting the second path down to a final X ending location. These paths are located close to the fist to show it is connected to the object as the topic! All of these forms and their usage will be discussed in this book.

Mallory, Comparing the Egyptian, Arapaho linear, Arapaho, Chinese old and Chinese new style in that order. The simple fact that here are 5 written languages mixed with the understanding that they appear similar in drawn representational form, including linear, is further proof the simplistic forms of sign, written and petroglyphs symbols can be the same and even look the same! Along with these symbols, Mallory outlines exactly how the sign movements are done for each, looking exactly like the drawings. Referencing his own scientific statements in the book on sign coming before tongue and written languages, the similarity of the written is BASED off of the sign language version. If the opposite is argued, then the sign is based off the written! Either way works for me that you choose. Simply put, there is more compelling evidence in these 4 global written languages combined with the sign movements of these in these cultures, than in all the evidence AGAINST this being connected!

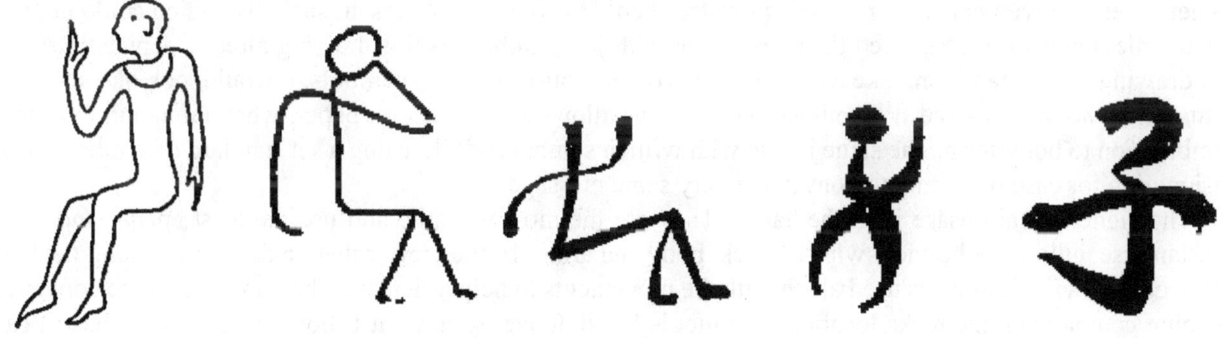

Visual Stimuli

So many images flood our life now and more are on the rise, because marketers found out something. What? The fact that humans associate quicker and buy more from visual stimuli! *Mallery, Sign Language Among North American Indians Compared With that among other peoples and deaf-mutes first annual report of the bureau of ethnology to the 1881. pointing at objects and making gesticulations, pg 427 states;*

"Whether or not sight preceded hearing in order of development, it is difficult, in conjecturing the first attempts of man or his hypothetical ancestor at the expression either of percepts or concepts, to connect vocal sounds with any large number of objects, but it is readily conceivable that the characteristics of their forms and movements should have been suggested to the eye fully exercised before the tongue so soon as the arms and fingers became free for the requisite simulation or portrayal."

Commercials submerge us in the slow images of burgers and car body lines to entice you to buy one compared to reading English language across a screen! Saying a hamburger is delicious has been replaced by media today by simply showing a juicy hamburger image. Thus bypassing the effort of reading boring wordage and stimulating the brain directly with images of the food. A viewed language is just more artistic and fun because our brains stimulate easier with visual representations quicker! More has been learned about learning in the last ten years than all previous years combined! Modern school processes have went to a more pictorial process using technology. As Mallery stated earlier, the possibility that simply because of the amount of nerves going from the eye to the brain makes it obviously the choice of learning ability over all others! It is thought that the mind remembers 90 gigabits of data daily! And that a human witnesses, visually, well over 200 gigabits of data a day the brain must filter! Compared to other duller senses this is obviously more data influencing your lives and thus focus on visible light has been applied by our brains since eyes were developed.

Body Dexterity

A viewer is needed to witness sign language to understand the language in real time, unless you use petrography! A signer is needed, who uses motion from the torso from the waist to the head. With full articulating arm movement ability from the torso to above the head in variable sweeping arcs and be able to sign in a forward direction to the outstretched straight armed position as the maximum limits of the bodies ability to articulate. The signer can also move his head side to side, front to back, and rotate it left and right. The signer has some facial movements that assist in the story telling. The main torso of the signer can swing slightly in a rotating horizontal direction as well.

Again if you observe Mallory's image of a sign language body position and movement designated by various symbols to depict arm travel, hand stopping and position to body and secondary movement down of the arm to a position starting from the hand and arm against the body in a specific way, to an outstretched arm slightly higher. Then a movement down remaining outstretched! If you were not present such discussion could not take place, unless you simply replaced the man's form with just symbols as this drawing already depicts! Because just drawing the human form, take away Mallory's other motion and stop symbols, it would look like an Indian sitting there holding his chest! Combination drawings allows you to see, on paper, what animation existed in combination to body form. The same is true with written symbols of UL, using a set standard of symbology for designation for ease of writing to convey the very same message.

The signer's main usage is in the hands. They are the most versatile and use the least energy and allow constant use, unlike the heavier swing of neck, body and arms. To the viewer there exists levels along the head to lower torso visible as areas used along with the movements to help articulate what is wanted to be conveyed. In some comparison, the rocks location of symbols listed above, somewhat follow these areas as best it can. There is the zone above the head, face, neck, shoulders, chest, abdomen and areas the arms can move around the body and in front of it. Little could be told with the arms behind the back as the viewer would not be able to see it! The original Universal Language exists mainly in what I call 1D modeling. This is the linear representation of the Sign version of the UL. Later cultures used what I call 2D modeling, having linear styling that is drawn with hollow form outlined with linear lines giving body to the subjects. And then a highly artistic representation of the 1D and 2D models in what I refer to as 3D, having intricate artistic representations and very detailed features. The Incas used 3D style such as open lips drawn to represent a hole or cave, instead of a circular line curved to look like a cave.

I will be displaying the original 1D style mainly. But to understand the symbols, some discussion into the body movements that originally created the written dialect must be understood. From these movements, like the natural movements I discussed above, some symbols can be generated just by drawing the movements of the sign and BEFORE you ever find such a symbol! Backward engineering, if you will is the best way to generate extra symbols that may exist. These symbols generated this way may be close to the actual symbology if you run across it later. Trying to turn symbols into body movements to recreate sign language is another technique that may help you determine if you are correct in your original assessment of it's meaning. If it is found similar to other determined symbol meanings you may have to reconsider it's meaning.

Once you accept the symbology as language you can then consider that many symbols exist undiscovered! If there is a symbol for fire, then there must be a symbol for smoke? What about fog or temperatures, weather, and sickness. Everyday life situations must have symbols attached specifically or the language would be somewhat worthless. Knowing this, goes a long way in your skill building and help you gain momentum in the vast Universal Language. Plate #4 shows the viewers perspective of the signers body movements and hand and wrist articulation.

Attached to this is your first look at a 1D style Human (man) form symbols in different configurations. A few obvious symbols for Man and Woman can be figured out without drawing them and is important to many sites. There are countless other human form symbols and you should make a listing of them as you go as I am teaching the ancient language and not writing a complete dictionary of every symbol form. You will quickly realize the linear 1D human form has a head, body, legs and arms. Simply put your body in these positions to quickly figure out they are the natural movements we use as humans. You must also, and more importantly, recognize that the body, arms, legs and attachments are comprised of the PATH and POINT core symbols of your finger! They are just placed in a man configuration to instantly give you the complete understanding that they are describing a human and what is going on with that human!

You have now advanced from a core symbol understanding into applying those core symbols into human life events specifically. You will immediately understand they are not talking about a dog, a bird, a rock, the stars, the weather or other environmental things! They are symbolizing about what happened to someone or a group. I listed some complex symbols attached to the body so you may start to develop more advanced understanding of how symbols are connected in many different ways to add even more information that would be unable to be understood with just the body symbols. Remember that the human form symbol combinations are specifically talking about the human and not the environment. Keep them separated in your mind, because other symbols are used for that. The human form is the most important of symbols usually drawn to show an action or connection from the man to the area, task, or event. Sometimes you can completely decipher all the other symbols and then run across the human form in the panel and it really completes the understanding, or completely changes it! Human form is very prolific, but site for site other symbols are listed more so human forms are a prize to find indeed. At that point you know there is probably an action you can do here or that has been done instead of just environmental data recorded or other non-interactive information listed. Sometimes the hardest part of the human symbol is deciding it is a human form symbol! They can be stretched across an entire large panel and you think at first it is something else entirely: so small or just the upper torso listed that you miss it. As a helpful note, each site should be photographed and what I do is print out panels I cannot decipher and put them in a book to look at again and again when I am bored. In this way, my mind can internalize the symbols and as the years go by sometimes separate them into understanding. The main thing when you fail decipher or hit the wall, coming back to the image after time has passed allows you to see it in a different way.

Sometimes confusion can happen with much detail added, or included as time goes on at a site through the years, the writer attempts to minimize that by clearly depicting information related to a specific story or flow of stories meant to go together so the user can read it. Other stories and topics should be written separately to again help in simplicity. Another trait used everywhere is the symbols ability to be written in different ways to say the same thing! The writer should and usually does draw the topic again and again in several ways on the same panel so the user can quickly get the understanding of the story, another important fact you must remember to advance.

Note the second to last symbol of "holding back movement and talking about it" is showing a spiral above it which I will explain in a later chapter. Sometimes these symbols are combined with more than the human figure and include a tail on the human as seen in the 4th form in the 3rd row. These tail forms are represented from an animal in nature that uses it's tail distinctly in different situations and thus easy to mimic for human actions of the same nature! That animal is the dog.

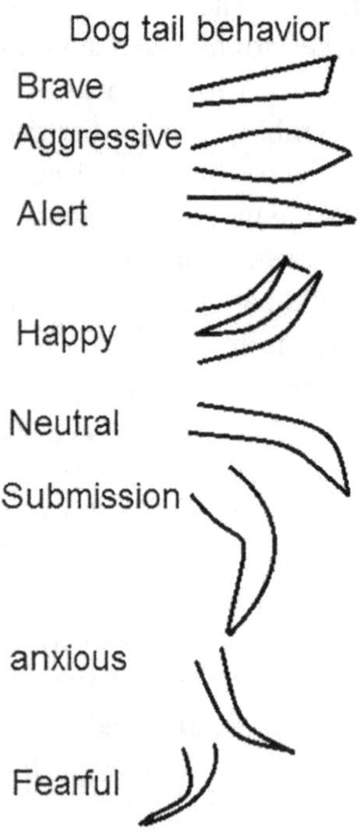

Plate #4

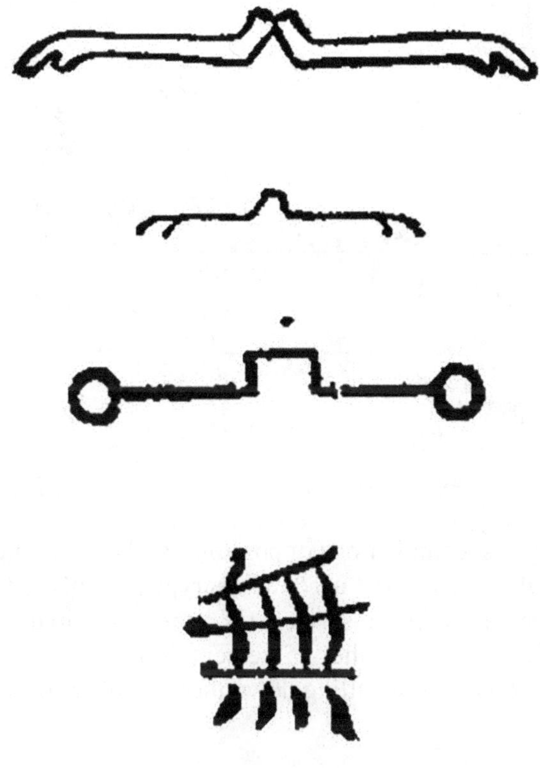

Plate #5

Mallery, Garrick (2009-10-04). Sign Language Among North American Indians Compared With That Among Other Peoples And Deaf-Mutes First Annual Report of the Bureau of Ethnology to the ... ... Office, Washington, 1881

Negation/Nothing drawn images for similarity of cultures written language. In order, Egyptian, Indian, Mayan and Chinese (metacarpal bones shown in the work).

Noting Mallory again, Indian positioned and drawn with hand to breast then up and out to a fist in a sweeping path, then down to a stopping point to designate sign language movements. As petroglyph symbols represent.

Core starter symbols

Learning the basics is key to reading a language that is based off of man's natural movements and mimicked from the natural world around them. The steps to be taught include:

1. One basic key is to understand the physical limits of man's body movements.

2. Then to understanding the usability of a visual system that can be mimicked by man or left in solid form on a rock or hide.

3. Lastly is on to the core story setup, symbol structure and finally advanced combining of symbols.

One page from my log of my first compilations of possible symbol meanings. These referenced any and all sources including my own thoughts when I first used my encryption skills to try and bust the code after about 5 years of researching sites in earnest after the service. Of my entire initial archive of 600 plus symbols and groups over half were completely wrong! Another 25 percent do not even exist as an independent symbol or group and still 5 percent are unknown. But whittling down these numbers only led to more being added which are unknown and rare.

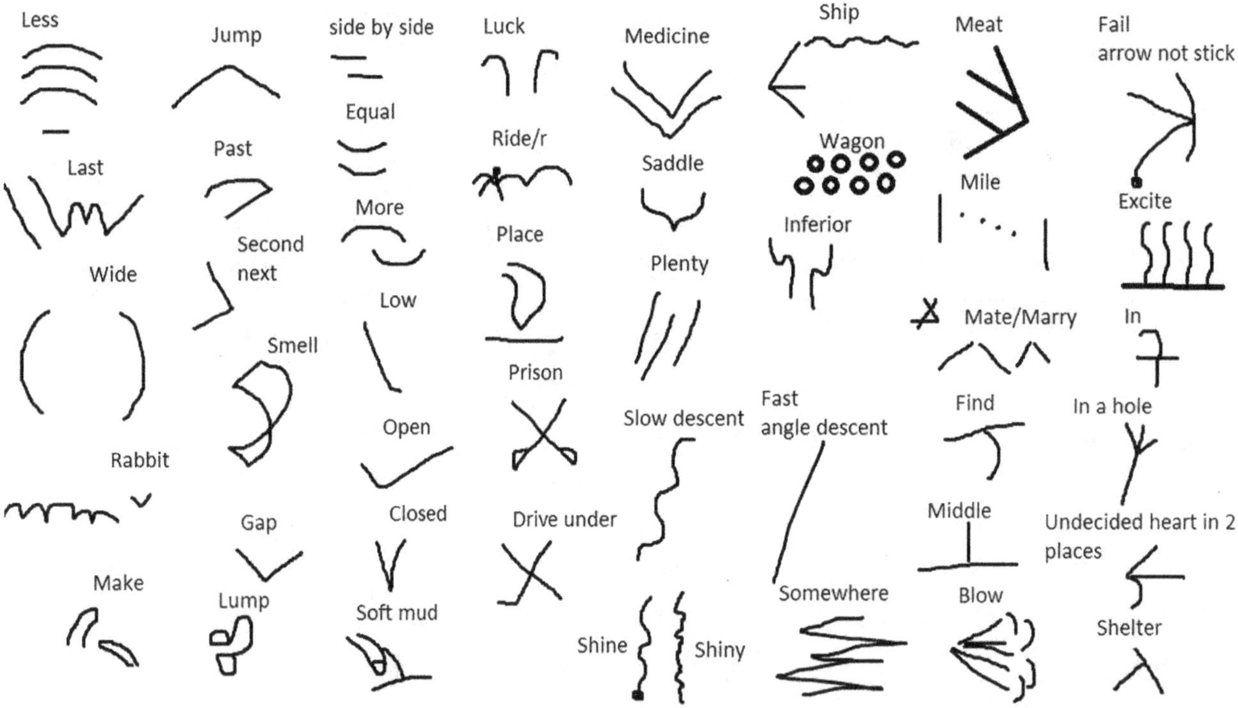

Here is one of many lists I compiled while doing research strictly using forms of sign language and how the body movements could possibly be drawn into symbol form to represent a meaning. How many are proven out? 1 so far! The Excite symbol group appears to be correct to date. Which uses the flat hand in front of you at low torso level with semi open fingers, palm up and where one moved his hand upward while waving it slightly back and forth while doing so to indicate "excitement". Every other one has either not been discovered in the field or is still undecided upon. Most of these are strictly Path symbols and thus fall into a vast arena of differing meanings and is the biggest compiled group of meanings in the U.L.

Hand Movement

Basic ancient petroglyph language is based off of THE Ancient Universal Sign Language. Ancient sign language is based off of nature and the body's natural movements controlled by the brains thought process to convey meaning using what body parts you have that the intended audience can observe These movements would primarily come from the hands and arms, then the torso, head and expression. It must first be taught in sign language that all human conceptual understanding by visual means mixed with sound, expression, body gestures and lastly some learned movements designated for specific explanations. These are easier if the movements smoothly follow natural gestures easily mimicked by the human body! The easiest way to complete this task the fastest is of course just point with your index finger of your hand! It feels natural, it is natural, and your brain is so accurate using this technique it can angle your finger to amazing accuracy no matter where you hold your hand out, even out of alignment with your eyes to the object! This is an amazing capability and has obviously required usage for primitive survival of our species. Any viewer can instantly know what you are trying to convey with no words! We use this sign language so much every day, we are actually skilled at it and teach through society many types of movements for different reactions you are trying to emphasize! Think of when you hold open the palms of your hands in front of you with fingers open in a display of "nothing in my hands" when you emphasize physically a question you ask someone on a topic you're trying to gather an answer on or answering someone with a "I don't know" reply!

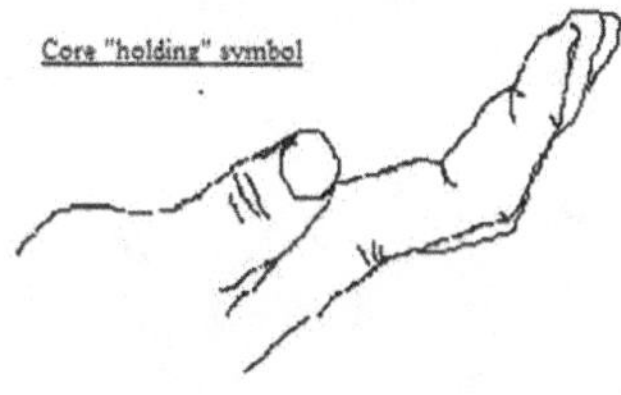

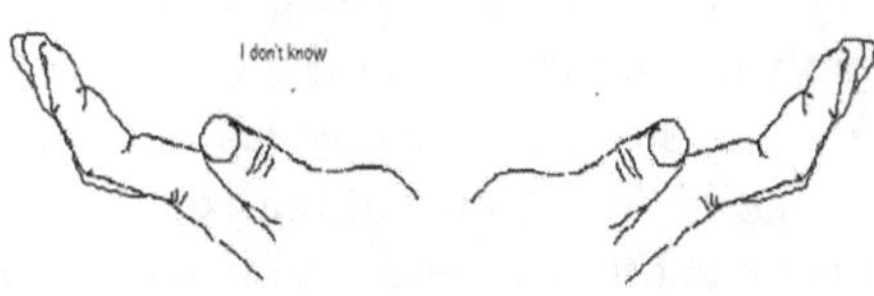

Your body automatically emphasizes your reply without you sometimes even having to state you don't know! Your body is asking for a mental filing of knowledge duplicated in a physical sense of putting something in your hands by outreaching them to show your brain does not know the answer and looking for a handout of knowledge! This is An interesting gesture from your brain to represent a non-physical request or response into a physical act by your body's reaction. Your brain relates not knowing an answer as emptiness, just the same as your empty hands void of a physical substance! It knows someone cannot see in your head so the hands having nothing in them are something a viewer could see. Your brain is projecting physically from your body to ASSIST the viewer what you know. This shows a natural act of wanting to communicate with others.

You are using sign language passed on by everyone around you, but why? Why can't you just state it? Because your brain is not confined to just a tongue, it utilizes all of you all the time. First sign started from the most basic gestures and our hands are most able to do these gestures. Your face would get tired only gesturing and use extra energy. Your brain realizes this and instead uses your hands as they are the best able to perform so many articulations. So naturally sign language began using mostly hand gestures, then it was mixed with arm movements to move your hands into positions and directions to further compound movement. Using the least amount of energy allows signing ability to increase many fold. Some movements can be incorporated with lesser movements of the torso, head and facial expressions.

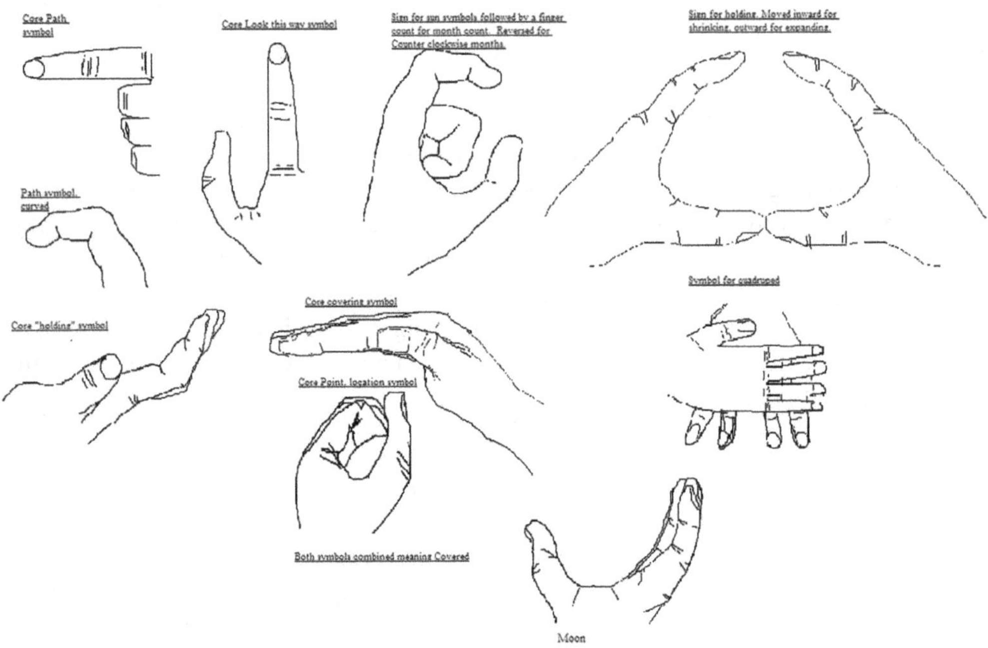

You have just learned the most basic symbols of all petroglyph language! All other forms of ancient writing is based off these two raw symbols. You also learned the first connection of the two. Your fingers thin length is a "Path". The tip of your finger is the "Point". You used it to show the physical path to an object, and in actuality your brain can easily guide and understand that your finger is shorter than the path, but that the tip of your finger is closest of your body to the object and therefore designates your fingertip as the object location. Thus making the simple combination of the path extending from your eye to the object location designated as the single point! The dot at the ending represents a very physical object, whereas the path is an imaginary line generated from your eye to the object. Path is then simply movement! A dot is more simply a physical location. Being opposites makes the writing system usable as all things human are physical or stationary and/or seen in movement. Just point at somebody to know how they take it! The "path" along your finger is not an issue, but the end of your finger closest to their nose is surely the object they object to you aiming at them! Of course a path like a highway can be a physical object, and a point can be other than a physical object. They can even be both. A point of light could be a star and the light is the topic, which has no human physical mass to touch and thought of as not physical, yet it is generated by a physical star! Those differences must be able to be conveyed effectively.

Finger Path and point diagram

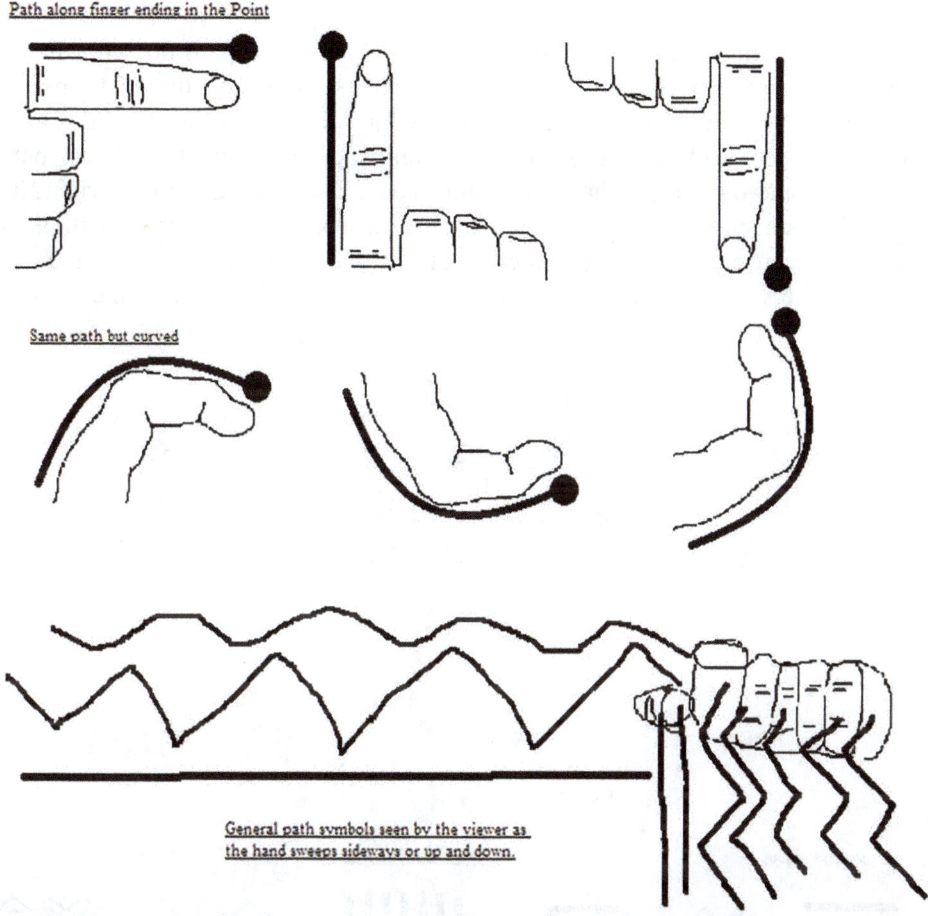

Symbol Categories

There are many symbol categories to cover which can never be completed in this book. I will cover some of the important ones and just touch others I hope to expand on later. There are some symbol groups I am not completely sure on and will not try and give bad direction on until I prove them out more. I will try and comment on some in this category as we come across them to give my thoughts on what they COULD be, but I will include that statement when I am not sure. The decipherment of a language lost for thousands of years by every human is not something I can completely crack in my 40 years of interest, but I do hope to make more leaps in understanding as the years go by. My children appear to have much interest in the topic and hopefully will continue my adventures and decipherment movement for years to come. For now I can publish a most fantastic deep look into the most important symbols used by man and left by ancient man with blood, sweat, and tears to tell us now! That message is important indeed and we must take notice, or at least individually take interest to give us another tool of survival, if shit ever hits the fan and your life may depend on the information of nature contained in the rock libraries of the world! Let us begin.

Core Symbol Paths and Points

The path begins as your finger, as a straight solid line ______. But a path does not have to be straight obviously, it can be bent^, circled(), squiggly~, dashed ----, reversed], arced(, turned[], flowing~~, crooked/, equal=,bumpy^^^^, wavy~~~, thick- and thin-. So everything drawn can be a path! Except a DOT- the POINT. A point is the physical spot the path starts, ends, jumps to, or doesn't include the path at all. But in every path there is a point or two because it has a start and an end. Except for a CIRCLE right? There is no start or ending with a circular path symbol. So including a circle as a separate core symbol with the path and point is not really appropriate because it is a path, just a cycle of continuous movement. So in the most basic of UL symbol learning there is the single core image- the Path or the Point '._.' as seen in the finger path and point diagram above.

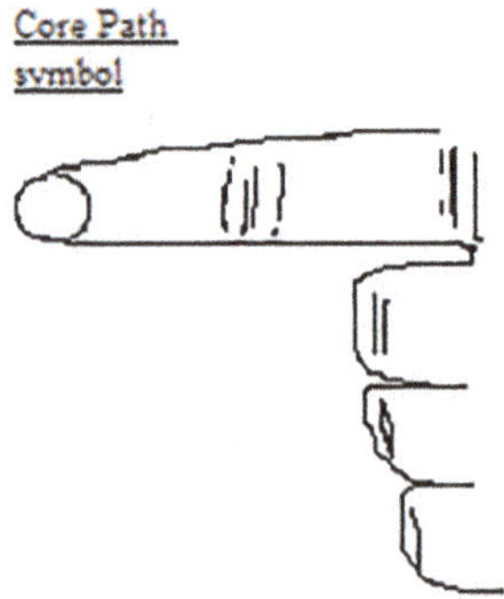

Plate #3

Multiple Symbols

The next step in UL writing is the MULTIPLE symbols. These include simple combinations of symbols of the same type (all Paths or all Points). The = equal sign is a great multiple symbol image combining two exact core paths together. >, + or . is another few symbols combined to make multiple sets.

Complex Symbols

The next step in UL writing is the COMPLEX symbols. These have more than a few core combinations and get into differing combinations. >< or * or # is more complex than simple few symbols and could be very large continuations along a panel. Concentric circles and spirals really fall into this type of writing.

Combined symbols

Next up in UL writing is COMBINED symbols. :> would be a combination of points and paths. Combinations start pulling away from Core Symbol forms and gets into more specific symbol pairs dedicated to specific meanings! A problem with sign language simple using single letter sign to spell out everything the user tries to get across is that it would take forever! So the great thing with sign, is one can break off specific hand movements (thus creating fixed combinations of symbols to relate to those movements) to depict whole topics with much less energy and time required! One could always go back to the basics and sign independent symbols to get the same thing, which brings me back to what I said earlier that there are many ways to depict a theme in writing UL.

Symbol use similarity requirements

The thing to remember about UL symbol decipherment is that the CORE symbol meanings should remain the basics of the final combination chosen for the topic! So if I were to draw a sunrise and sunset symbol set, the sun rise core path should be similar to a "cycle" and "rising" and the sunset should be the opposite. If the sunrise was made from descending symbols in their core meaning, it would be confusing and not transferable into sign language and therefore could not be correct in its meaning.

Natural Environment

Let's imagine what happened under the ancient glacier ice during the last ice age to begin the journey into the physical environment creation. And then why certain rocks were used for petroglyphs.

. A microorganism grew under the ice on rocks and left a black coating on them when the ice receded. During that time the black did two things, it was very shiny and in the white background was very visible. The most important thing was it allowed solar energy to melt snow on it faster, other rock colors were used when black was unavailable. The petroglyph carvings in that time were also very brightly covered to stand out even more, unlike the dull and sometimes hard to view symbols today due to the countless years of weathering. Patination in the weathering environment after the ice age encrusts the rocks with a dark mineral which can recover the carved areas contrasting. Sometimes this layer can be looked at scientifically in thickness compared to non-carved areas of a rock to decide if age exists.

Rock Incorporation

The rocks physical design the symbols are carved on is very important. Chosen from the local environment to depict more of the story by the use of "rock incorporation". A fancy saying to mean using the natural cracks, divots, angles and locations on the rocks to enhance the understanding of the story being told. Unless there is only one rock to choose from, writing locations were chosen very carefully. The rock layout had as much to do with the message as did the symbols! I will enhance your knowledge on advanced topics of rock incorporation in further chapters, but suffice to say these rock incorporation tactics are the single most important topic about petroglyph writing because the designer always used it. My intuition about how a writer felt seeing that a rock resembled a given topic he was thinking to draw, it uncanny similarities to the event built into the rocks design naturally, I believe made the merging of the story to the rock almost a symbiotic and spiritual destiny of that writer to nature! And that he must have felt somewhat compelled to write it once the "story" showed itself to him on the rocks face. The writers skill in envisioning and extracting, in his mind, the story lines from the rock surface and then enhancing that rock to tell the whole story was a true showing of the brilliance of man. Which brings us to the written story setup upon the rock surface.

Symbol Meanings

Plate #5 explains the symbol meaning in Plate #3, which described the types of paths and points exclusively. Real meanings to some basic symbols built from core symbols usable in your travels to these sites. Remember from above that many factors can modify these symbols and groups by using thin or thick lines, dotted or dashed, scratched or otherwise make a huge determination in what the writer was conveying. Remember the writer did not mess up and accidentally draw these lines sloppy! If they curve and then thicken, that is the way the writer was drawing it. The use of sketching in the initial panel with charcoal prior to scratching or pecking before making it permanent allows very detailed and precise drawing for the user before creation.

You will see some very well used symbols for weather in the plate. These are important in most panels dealing with growing crops, hunting, occupation and travel. Less important in war story accounts. We will go over these symbols much more throughout the book. But to begin to see the information contained in most petroglyph sites it is important to understand that weather is a crucial part of human life and one of the most needed data items to track for fishing, hunting, war, travel, trade, crop growing and living times in a specific spot. Going back to the keystone rock layout you will notice weather is located usually above and to the right of the panel. There are obviously many changes for locations on panels throughout the world for weather but if the main story is for crops and foods for such things as deer migration hold over locations, the panel should be setup with the sky information above higher on the rock to designate clearly it is talking of the sky (Rock Incorporation). Remaining above symbols such as animals and food properly sets this data in connection with the animals and food to remain consistent UL practice. This also means, since the data is not centered, it is Data and not the main topic which is normally centered. So in these instances the animals or food supply is the main topic the panel is focused on. Unless the panel is completely dedicated to weather tracking, or some large flood or snowfall did damage, it always remains as secondary data. Knowing this in UL understanding helps you immediately decide if what the panel is about and if it is useful to you in what you are looking for, be it research or survival.

There are many bracketed (explained later in Bracketing) weather data panels that include weather in ongoing paths across the rock in layers all the way to the bottom of the rock. In these cases the entire panel is usually dedicated to weather information only to avoid confusion and thus NOT be used for sun position tracking. It may only use the different levels of shadow/light sun tracking lines going in a general trend across the rock to represent weather data directly on the sun symbols and along the paths that the rock was chose for in the first place, due to the direction and angle being suitable to track such events. These types of weather trend rocks were found to have a tracking shadow ability throughout the time cycle of the year and used accordingly to accurately depict ongoing weather patterns. Realizing the difference of the panel use is important if you are to decipher the area's use this panel assists in and avoid over-researching a panel for the wrong reason. I will show examples of these sun shadow rocks but for now it is important to explain differences to the basic panel data locations if the opportunity for the drawer existed where much more data is needed to be drawn and the simple top right quadrant of a rock does not allow for such!

Now is a good time to show some obvious weather trends you see today to better understand symbol combinations. You should have stood in the rain, snow and wind in your life and seen lightning and heard thunder in a storm. Have you seen lightning without a storm? Maybe in a volcanic eruption but obviously you need a storm to have the lightning. You will see more rain in Spring, less in Summer and more snow in Fall and Winter. The obvious trends of nature are easy to link to a time of the year, and sometimes to very exact times of the year. These weather data panels are meant to relay the locations specific weather patterns to better attempt to make better choices related to times so that the site may yield better results for the occupants, whatever that may be. So remember your real life experiences when dealing with glyphs and think about what you may require for information when reading a glyph site and you will grow your interpretational skills much faster.

You will find some sites with numerous rocks designating years of weather tracking information because the initial rock was overloaded with drawings. Some rocks are so over drawn that the original art is then re-drawn deeper or larger lined to again be brought to the front to be read because the old information changed or was less important and even confused the users! Another reason why "styles" of glyph writing is not a proper discipline and has nothing to do with the information contained. The labor of drawing such work on rocks is hard and no more labor than needed was used to project the simple information, baring the beautiful artistic representational thought put into some sites I should add. Those types of sites were drawn from a very dedicated drawer and many of the more holy sites are depicted with artistic representation. General sites with simple data written do not need such artwork. Graveyards are another place that use heavily artistic representations because it is their loved ones.

Let us look at the symbols in Plate #5 specifically. There are path symbols used just slightly different to make different meanings. The cliffs symbol for instance. It is a row of single paths straight up (like a cliff) but usually no top line, as that is used as the sky. I have seen where the rock structure, like up on a top edge, might be scraped to designate the user is using the rock to depict the top of the cliff, thus using the rock texture incorporation to define the information better. Now simply adding a line above it changes it from a rocky cliff to rainfall! Angle the path lines sideways and you have a windy rain. Zigzag them along the path and you have the gentle fall patterns of snowflakes. Cross them and you have fog. You can quickly see why I say symbol combinations in many forms are combined and used for specifically one meaning. An angled cliff may be drawn sideways like hard rain but it would be in an obvious setting, so the reader understands completely the difference. Usually, you can rely on the fact each symbol of the UL is designated for the specific meaning you will normally see on a panel. In this way it is assured information can be read much quicker and so the inventors of the UL, which must have taken much time, incorporated these final symbol combinations for normal encountered things you will run into in life.

The next subtle change needing recognized is the sideways paths. Look at the mountain range, water waves and water springs and snowpack. Remember to use real life experiences to figure out the slight differences and why they exist. Water makes gentle flowing rounded turns, like a river or spring going downhill. Think of mountain ranges and the sharper edges of each mountain. Waves of a lake are rounded but have more layers of waveforms so combining wave forms in layers shows it is a body of water, not just a spring path. Mountains are the same, a single mountain or string of hills together will just have one sharp pointed zigzag line. A range will have multiple layers of lines stacked.Notice the flooding path from the rain clouds converting from a diagonal angled downward pointing rain symbols to flatter and snaking lines to show it floods. Snow lines (layers) below the snow shows pack height, usually in actual pack height drawn right on the rock of the height of the snow level. Combinations of all weather is seen in the storm symbols combining everything at once. An earthquake, depending on movement direction and type, can be shown with bumpy waveform paths, flowing, sharp waves and so on. Giving the user of UL to draw limitless types of information of shake and movement of anything with fair detail to include counts and times of that movement or reoccurrences!

Another point worth noting here is the "bad" symbol. It is comprised usually of a fully drawn in symbol to show it is covered with something. Such coverage usually representing blood, which is always bad, covering the surface of your skin to designate bad or unhealthy and such drawing in is harder than a simple outline and only used to represent when needed. Another use is to show the path or direction is bad or "full" or filled in and impassable or a bad direction.

Rain into Ice

The specific instance of turning liquid water in the form of rain into ice in symbol form is an educational look into UL ability to adapt a Core set of symbols to mean both the same thing as it did and to also mean something beyond the basic designation related to the core value, like rain and ice, both being water but in different states.

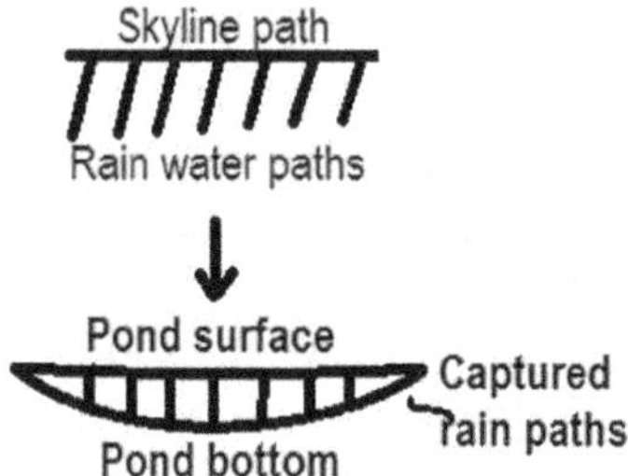

The neat thing with the frozen symbol is the symbol of a generic outline of a ponds surface and bottom (curved) to also be the containment lines for the interior water path lines! Thus the symbol group uses the least amount of written design to get across the meaning.

The fact that the frozen symbol group does not designate using captured flowing water like a spring's curving path is highly relevant as the flowing curves would mean captured water able to move (in other words it would then mean a lake and not ice). Straight, and usually vertical only, lines like rain show a more fixed adjustment compared to the slightly curved rain paths usually seen in panels. A more vertical rain path always designates the ability of the storm to sustain continuous, though lower yield, rain over a period of time whereby ever increasing angle of rain drop path lines shows the tendency of storm movement. As does that angle show the increased winds, blowing the rain sideways, and since both natural events are present in a moving of the storm and the speed of the movement, both are another flexibility and harmony of UL to designate multiple natural happenings at the same time with just a single drawn symbol! We could go on to include the lengths of the rain paths and the frozen pond for more or less water and more or less surface of the water in a flooding state, but suffice to say the ICE symbol group is the perfect teaching item to show the flexibility of UL drawing variation from the core value to more complex meanings, yet in the purest sense still means the core definition!

Circles

The circle is the third and final basic Core symbol, a looping path, having no start or end. It represents "captured" and held in place. Like the core path along the straightened finger and the fingers end, the circle is a continuation of that theme. In the most core sense, again using the fingers Path line curved, the circle represents the most basic core value of a path, just looping continuously. The path simply converges using the fingertip and the thumb tip touching each other in a "pinching" manner against each other to hold something. This is the core sign for the circle

Circle creation
touching tips.

symbol. Unlike the solid form point symbol, the circle is more open, but remains round to show the path existing around the circumference of the touching points of the finger and thumb. Meaning in the core sense "to hold", "hold here" and "held in place" the basic meanings focus around the natural grasping of the finger and thumb. Very different in meaning, the point symbol being in the center of this location designating the physical location but not being constrained, the circle designating the act of being held.

To sum up the differences of the three core symbols you can now see that all three come from the finger alone. From these spread out the entire Universal Language. Like pronunciations of Latin varies, the basic sound still matches the alphabetic symbol and is tied to it just like UL. The fingers length represents the path, an open flowing direction of travel. The tip of the finger is the end of the path and thus the point designates a physical location, able to be an ending point, a starting point and thus a designator usable as "First" (beginning). The circle represents the fingers ability to Hold and thus is representing holding something physical. The expanded representation can then be used to show a physical object and can even designate an object. All three symbols thus cover basic requirements to designate all things in nature as a language in a 3 dimensional world. The understanding of a physical location, the human ability to interact with nature and the human mobility in that environment.

Seasons

Is the symbology of the first language starting to be comprehended? You haven't learned anything yet, let's begin!

What good is all this data without understanding the relationship to time? Cassiopeia and the moon is great, but the Sun is the definitive yearly precession counter. Sun tracking was one of the most important and prolific events throughout the globe and the seasons were very important for obvious survival reasons. At one point I could read panels, but could not specify any type of date. Later I could read star systems and could identify possibly that they tracked time in this way both thru the night and year, but unable to collaborate it. The moon remained elusive, but started to take shape in the week tracking bars discussed earlier. It would be 20 years later and hundreds of site visitations before the breakthrough happened and I could read what season was described! I thought then, what more could you want to know once you can read and identify what the season was when they used the site? Because if you think of the 4 seasons, you have a lot of the required knowledge usable to migrate, know crop cycles and so on! I began to realize, in reality, for an ancient civilization the four seasons were the most important tracking of the yearly cycle and so the season group must be the most reduced delineation of the year they used. Simple start, middle and ending times of the seasons could be marked if really needed. Breaking the year into four parts for Winter (hibernation and cold), Spring (warming, rain and bloom), Summer (growing and hot) and Autumn (harvesting and cooling).

Core Combinations

The need to designate a fixed symbol group for the sun and the seasons was imperative and one of the biggest mysteries in petroglyph understanding to all. The basic combination included the circle and the point.

Because the circle and the point combined together has other meanings in sign, it could not be used as the designator. So a second outer circle was incorporated into the grouping to form what is the FIXED base Season symbol representing the start of the "Season Symbol Group". Thus the Winter symbol was created!

The circles in this grouping represent the sun in its continuing and progressive changing arcs in the sky through the year. The shape of the circular journey of rotation around the planet keeping to the core "Path" of the circular symbol grounds it correctly with Core meaning. The circle in circle grouping makes a pattern that specifically designates and fixes it's form into that of the sun's Seasons in sign language. And thus the simple closing of the index finger to the thumb tip in an open circular form with the remaining fingers closed tighter inside the opening is the sign form of the sun.

Winter

The two circles are added to the single central point to designate "winter" and the winter solstice. The point represents a core symbol value again as a "fixed" position. In this case the fixed position means "first" and thus designates this winter symbol group as the "First Season" of the year (and the sun's first position of the year) and the fixed point designating the first solstice when the sun is at it's lowest in the sky and thus has the least amount of daylight hours of the year!

Spring

Next in the progression is of course Spring, so simply adding another ring makes the fixed symbol group designating Spring, and the first Equinox of the year when both the day and night have exactly the same hours! Again the central point symbol represents the first equinox and the first symbol of this group (as you will see the difference in the Autumnal symbol group below). It also assists in showing it is a larger symbol from winter and coming after winter is enlarged to show again that the sun is higher in the sky and thus has a longer arc path visible than in winter. The growing path of the sun's arc in the sky continues and thus the enlargement is also shown in the larger symbol. We will discuss this further in a minute.

Summer

Next season in the precession of the year is Summer, which is the highest and longest of the suns arc across the sky and so deserves the biggest symbol 4 complete circles! The point seen in the last winter and spring symbol groups has been "opened" and thus becomes a full circle, still able to represent a fixed spot in a core symbol sense but now used to show the largest of the sun symbol groups! As summer marks the Summer Solstice where the longest day of the year is marked and the sun is highest in the sky this symbol is largest as well.

Autumn

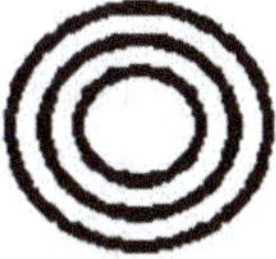

The most interesting of the season symbols is Autumn. This is because the sun's track is reducing and dropping in the sky from summer, thus the symbol is smaller. When the Autumnal Equinox comes, it again is the time when the equal time of day and night exists and thus is equal to the spring equinox! Except two important factors; the sun's arc is declining into winter from summer and thus is different than Spring, and that it is the second equinox of the year and coming after spring! So to represent both a larger symbol group than winter but less than the growing sun arc and height of the spring symbol group, three full circles are used! The dot is removed because it is not the first equinox, and the continued use of the three circles show equality and harmony of both the spring and autumn equinoxes and symbols that oppose each other yearly.

Nature Tied Symbols

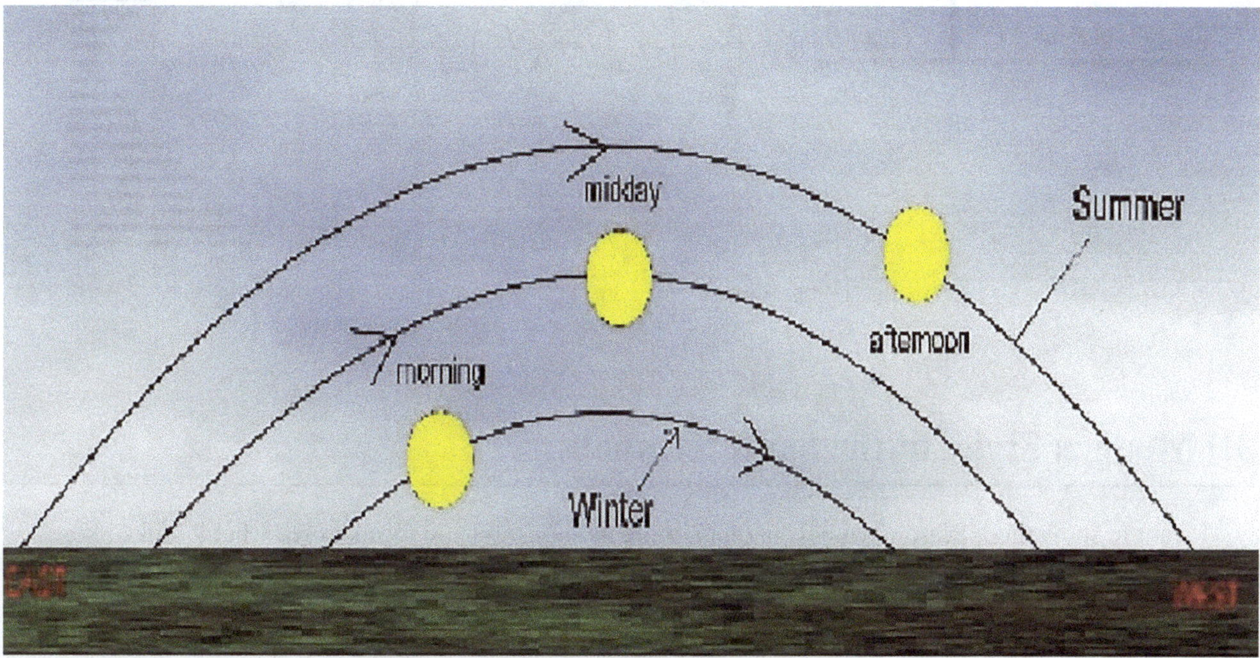

As represented in the image the sun's arc in the sky is lowest in winter and highest in summer with central height existing in both the spring and autumn equinox periods! If you combine these three arcs as circles in circles you create a similar looking existence to all the season symbols from smallest to largest.

A representation of how such sun movement creates a usable platform for petroglyph use by using the cast shadow movement. A stick represents the shadow caster and the shadow length can be recorded as shown. It is interesting the shadow trace is that harmony represented in the yin yang symbol.

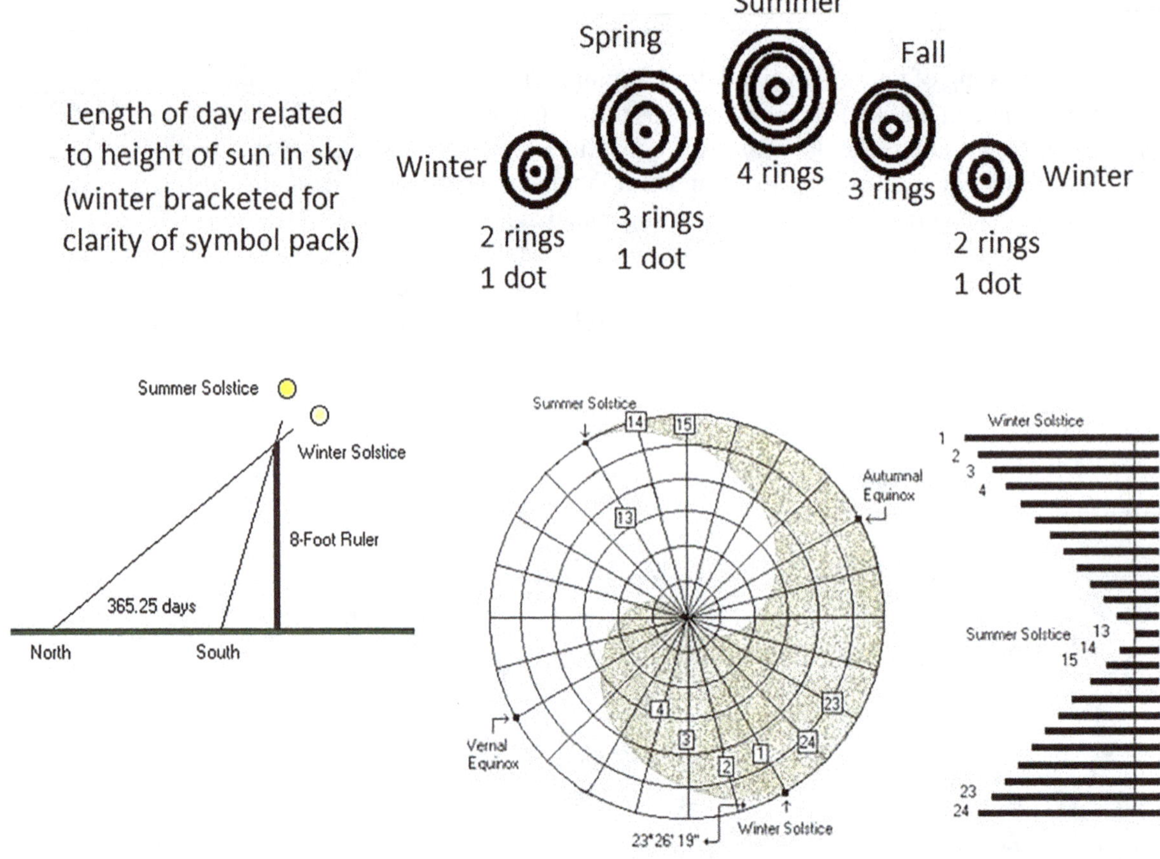

3D Modern Styles of the Same Symbols

I want to show these Season symbols in other, more modern, stylistic forms to see what it looks like.

"Big SunMan" by Gail Root of Deming, NM. A fantastic example of a 3D representation of a combined Season Symbol group. Note the straight shadow cast against the lines.

"Little SunMan" picture from Gail Root Deming, NM in the same combined symbol group panel group as Big SunMan above, but this panel is cast on by a remote rock outcrop with a square opening in it up the hill during the Summer and Winter Solstices! You can meet great folks like Gail Root and Logan Ray Bier who love petroglyphs on social media sites like Facebook Groups Nevada Backroads, Petroglyph of Nevada and Beyond, Petroglyphs, Pictographs, and Rock Art of North America and Explorers of Native American Rock Art!

The Little SunMan projection rock photo by Gail Root Deming, NM again, note the rock with Little Sun-Man panel on the opposite side of this photo is facing the keyhole square opening!
To sum up the modified symbols then, it can be represented as these symbols!

3D style Season Symbols

Contracting and Expanding Paths

Seen in the panel below, the sign language for compressing and expanding is by using the open circle paths made by the fingers and thumbs making an open circle touching each other (Plate #10). Then moving the hands inward to shrink the circle or outward to expand it. This is used in dealing with the season's beginning and ending cycles showing radiating lines (paths) to show the direction the symbol is growing or shrinking by placing the lines toward the inside or outside of the circle line. As the seasons are 3 months the first 1.5 months fall into expansion and the last 1.5 months declining. Usually the line numbers around the circle are in groups of 7 or 13, but could be more or less and used as small shadow paths for times designated.

Seasonal Day Counters

Like the moon count symbol group, there is the season count symbols. Directly linked and bracketing the month started in this panel at Signal Hill, Az. the count is an easy mark off of 10 days in the top circle in the image (the central dot open showing it is used as a count hegd this circle group is touching the path line from the month symbol in the center to where you start the count) to equal 1 mark off for a 9 count in the second circle (the lower circle with a solid center showing it is not used). When the 10 count is completed and each of the 9 segment is marked off with paint you have completed the 90 days between each season/solstice to equinox.

Shadow Rock Incorporation

You will notice on Figure #15 the circle is somewhat out of round. You will witness this often and corresponds to the shadow line that is cast onto the rock thus assisting understanding (and actual tracking of the time) with rock incorporation. We will get into plenty of that later.

Another look at the shadow line panel to clearly see the divided season symbols as they are related to the rock cast shadow through the year. The shadow cast outlines are highlighted with white and the rock lip outlined as the dark line.

Bracketing with Season Symbols

The start of ancient UL story panels usually start with the Eastern region of the rock and spreads toward the west! This again is due to the natural movement of the sun as it starts its day rising in the East and setting in the West. So depending on the direction of the panel this direction is not set as a right to left pattern but could very well be left to right or down to up! The start of a large story usually begins with "Brackets", those symbols which are usually Season symbols but could be simply single day symbols, a mix of Seasons and Months (all symbols explained in it's own chapters). These symbols are usually located close to each other with an open gap and a path line that encompasses the entire story by encirclement, or most of it, and is anchored by these bracketing symbols.

Here is a perfect panel bracketed (East being to the right), but much overwritten with data making it very hard to distinguish singular symbols to comprehend. The site is a place deer migrate to in fall and winter to stay due to ample food and water and pile in here once by the thousands, now by the hundreds. You can clearly see the Season Symbols used lower right in what is called a "Bracketing" of the story. You will see bracketing of a story a lot on keystone rocks, this is the main panel rock, all others are smaller stories. This shows the time between fall and winter use and broadens out in the surrounding paths to tell the complete story of food heights and many other topics including weather data listed above left and on this rock along the entire upper area of the rock. The brackets are lower right and are the start of the story and the ending!

Combining Different Season Symbols into One

Here is a panel in a site used for various activities in spring and fall! Combining the season symbols like seen here is common, but the outer ring is light and undefined more than the central rings, showing it designates a possible fourth ring. The heavy incised circles and dot are the focus of the times this site is occupied and represents the combined summer and fall usage seasons. Why not draw separate symbols for each season? Because these tasks were done in both seasons, thus being the same the combined symbol informs you of that. If the tasks were separate the symbols usually are separated or both tasks were "as important" and justified equality in your understanding of the site's usage. Another reason for combinations is if the rock shadow incorporation happens to give equal shadow casting within the same region, making it easy just to keep the original symbol and adding the combination symbol to the group.

Other Season References

The Universal Language was not just used as the rock writing of the ancients, it was used in the rock creations now known as Megaliths, scattered all over the world! The magnificent monuments, observatories and laboratories were built with the UL symbology INCORPORATED into them! Great online research can find hundreds of related Megaliths, geoglyphs and other massive sites.

Stonehenge Above, Photo by Photograph by Joe McNally/Sygma, from NationalGeographic.com

Full View of Gubekli Tepi illustration by Fernando Baptista , from webpage science.nationalgeographic.com/science/archaeology/photos/gobekli-tepe/

Photo and quote from Israel-Travel-and-Tours.com/rephaim.htm

"The Gilgal is the Israeli Stonehenge. The structure is composed of over 40,000 stones that are arranged in 4 circles. It is quite big – the diameter of the outer circle is about 150 meters/490 feet. The site is estimated to be 5,000 years old.

It is not totally understood what the purpose of the structure was. Some think it was a sort of a calendar or maybe a tomb or worship site.

Strangely enough it is best seen from above; however it sits on a plateau with no hills around it – which raises further questions regarding the purpose of the structure.

Gilgal or Galgal in Hebrew means a circle. Refaim means ghosts. But the Refaim were also a race of giant people that lived in the Bashan, which is the Golan of today. And they might just be the ones who built the place." End quote.

Shadow Lines

Like anyone with age, rocks have wrinkles! Usually big ones but they have them and the ancients used them to their advantage! They witnessed them casting shadows into fields where panels could be drawn and the yearly progression tracked by using these shadows as a time clock when it would hit the exact same spot each year.

The prior sun shadow line site of petroglyphs is best to describe what you will witness in sites dedicated mostly to the sun's yearly path. The season symbols can be seen on each level with a shadow line evident (highlighted by layers to show each area between the lines here). The Spring symbols and the days of the 3 months can be seen completely tracked along the shadows path. Seen is another half symbol used as a fixed sun marker designating a point in time is the elongated tall cover path symbol with a line in the center. You can see them side by side along the shadow paths used as count lines. The edge of another rock beside it is where the sun casts the shadow from onto this rock throughout this season. No, they are not vulvas or woman forms as many proclaim! Vulva forms do exist, usually on existing rock structures which mimic the form naturally, then enhanced further. In occasion they are used with the sun symbol form, to what end I do not know.

Daily Tracking Symbols with Shadow Lines

Notice the shadows point protruding and just missing the season symbol? This means the recorded date is not upon the site yet. But looking closely, you can see the tip of the shadow matches the shadow line under the circle exactly when it does line up.

Vertical Shadow Paths

Depending on the rocks shape the sun path may go upward! Notice the shadow "notch" residing on the general sun symbol where the radiating lines actually match the shadow angles exactly? This general sun symbol combination incorporating shadow lines around it defies the normal minimum cutoff of using more than one circle to signify the sun. Thus showing the context of the panel must be understood to properly interpret the symbol meaning due to the overlapping of the single circle symbol with other core meanings as mentioned earlier. A shadow path is usually present to assist in your decision but the best indicators are the shadow path radiating lines and their slight mis-alignment with each other as indicators that they were used to match a shadows edge. Note the vertical path sun tracking line, the offset angles each representing a progression in the yearly time marked when the sun shadow is cast upon that area of the path. Each of these steps has beside it a bit of data drawn showing what happens during that time of the year. Water overflow of the lakebed draining down the canyon is one event during snow melt in Spring.

Symbol Design Modified for Natural Shadow Shapes

Here another cast shadow tip (A) just missing the left ring the Season symbol (B), but the shadow extension that has a dip (D) nails center under the vulva form (sun day symbol) (C). Just to the right exists a zig zag (E) form that matches exactly with the arrow tip of the shadow (F) to further track progression of the shadow trend as it moves along. Look closely at the correlation of the left tip (A) of the shadows inward curvature which matches the season symbols outer circle size. These slight adjustments on the symbols on the rock in all these symbols is a direct modification to adjust them to fit the shadow lines exactly. You will have to realize these modification reasons sometimes without the shadows cast for comparisons but once you see why they did it the reason such changes are present is obvious.

Multiple Site Time Segmentation

I could fill the book with tracked shadows, the point is to show the use without a doubt. Never has the wrong symbols matched up with a shadow cast at the wrong time of year. These sites are used for tracking for tracking the year and should be visited and photographed. The phone sun location apps assist in this task instead of going to every site a lot each year. It also shows the reason for these sites. This also shows an occupation site is near for such long term tracking to happen regularly.

Month Symbols

For years after I cracked the season symbols I decided it was enough for ancient peoples to simply know the changing weather to the degree of the seasons only. Again I was thinking like scholars and ignoring what I knew that ancients were highly intelligent and smarter than that. I started to attack the presence of other symbols and time marks on season symbols to see how simple ways could be used to track more delineations of the seasons. What happened after was a progression of realizations that lead to a fascinating discovery- they used month symbols! All the modern knowledge written had many types of months for the year and numbers of months. Following a simple lunar cycle you count 13 months a year, but the ancients were smart and used 12 months just like we do.

Counting every symbol included in the Universal Language combined, I will never crack a more complex symbol group! I can understand how these symbols have eluded every human since the knowledge was lost. I now present the most amazing written connection to nature and the most beautiful of the Ancient Universal Language symbology!

Continuous Paths

I started understanding the month concept early on, but it mimicked the Season symbols so close I seen there might be a splitting of the seasonal 3 month segment by using two spiral forms, left and right twisting spirals! In the core sense a spiral is a continuous Path symbol and can mean to turn over if a single looping spiral is attached to something such as a dead body. A short loop spiral mimicked by sign language movement can denote, then, rotation which in turn includes the use of the concept beginning and ending (the start of the loop designates beginning and the end of the loop the ending). So as a core meaning the spiral represents a cycle and can expand to a fixed meaning with more spirals designating a set symbol group; having a beginning and ending. Thus having a dawning and setting like a solar day has, a lunar cycle, or the movement through a month. I originally took this as the dawning of a season and then the setting within the same season or another in the progression. This would account for similar spiral counts to the counts of the Season symbol group! Yet there was still count differences and sometimes more spiral data. Finally this progression of realization allowed me to see it was a monthly tracking symbol and visiting enough sites and researching prior sites I made the mighty connection I am very happy to find- each of the spiral symbols denotes a separate month on the natural yearly calendar of the sun! What is this natural calendar I refer to? Read on.

Spirals

A simple jaw line of a pyramid ancient sun serpent head of Quetzalcoatl of Mesoamerica showing a spiral. The serpent outline down the pyramid casts a shadow on the Spring and Autumnal equinox sunrise and sunset!

Analemma into Spirals

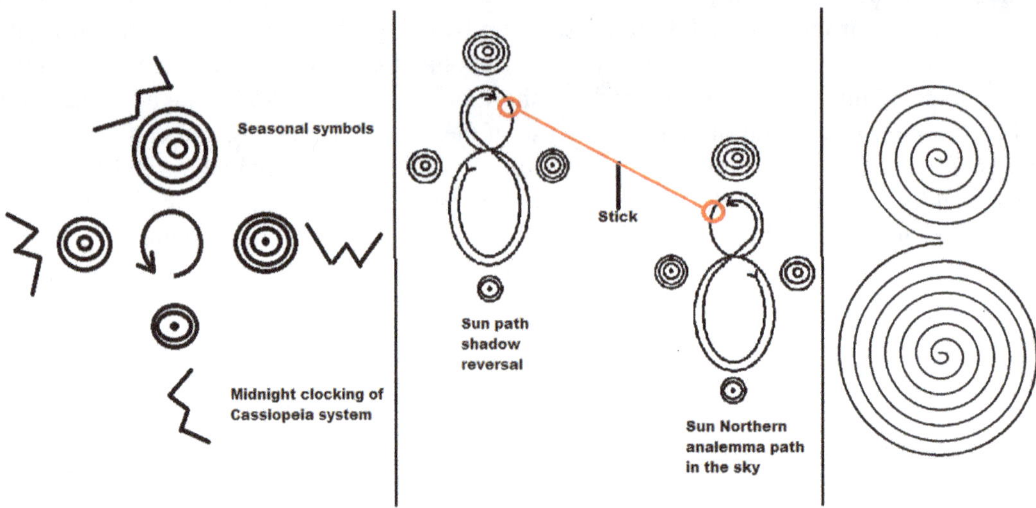

The analemma is the natural path the sun takes in the sky through the year and was used as a calendar in ancient times. It is a figure 8 the sun tracks in the sky and is made of a larger elliptical formed due to the slower moving sun track in the sky due to the greater distance from the Earth thru the Northern Hemisphere's colder months. And the smaller elliptic is due to the time the sun moves faster when the Earth is closest to the sun. Both due to the angle the sun hits as the tilt of the Earth changes this angle slightly as we circle the sun all year long. The sun, if marked at the same time every day, moves in this pattern and the season symbols are listed along this path to show you the locations above.

Shadows

Since it is hard to grab a visual reference staring at the sun in an empty sky, the ideal way to track this natural movement is by casting a shadow on the ground to mark the location daily. The shadow on the ground when using a shadow stick casts a reverse shadow direction, so what is seen in the sky is reversed on the ground.

Place that shadow path on a wall and you have a upside down version, in reverse. The very bottom of the path (the larger of the ovals) is Winter Solstice, at the top of the path (the small oval) is Summer Solstice. The center of the 8 is called the crossover and happens twice a year as the sun first crosses in Spring, and then crosses back over before Autumn. Midway on both sides of the lower, larger part of the elliptic path is the Equinoxes. The right column of plate shows the path lines in a continuous spiral direction with the inner path circles in the count equal to the months present in the top and bottom of the figure 8.

Direction of Spiral

The amazing thing with how they tracked time was to use this path the sun takes. The clever thing nobody realized was the fact they split the year and thus the months into the two DIRECTIONS OF ROTATION the sun path takes! So all of the months within each rotation starts the count (a spiral loop) from the first month and the count of more spirals increases with each month.

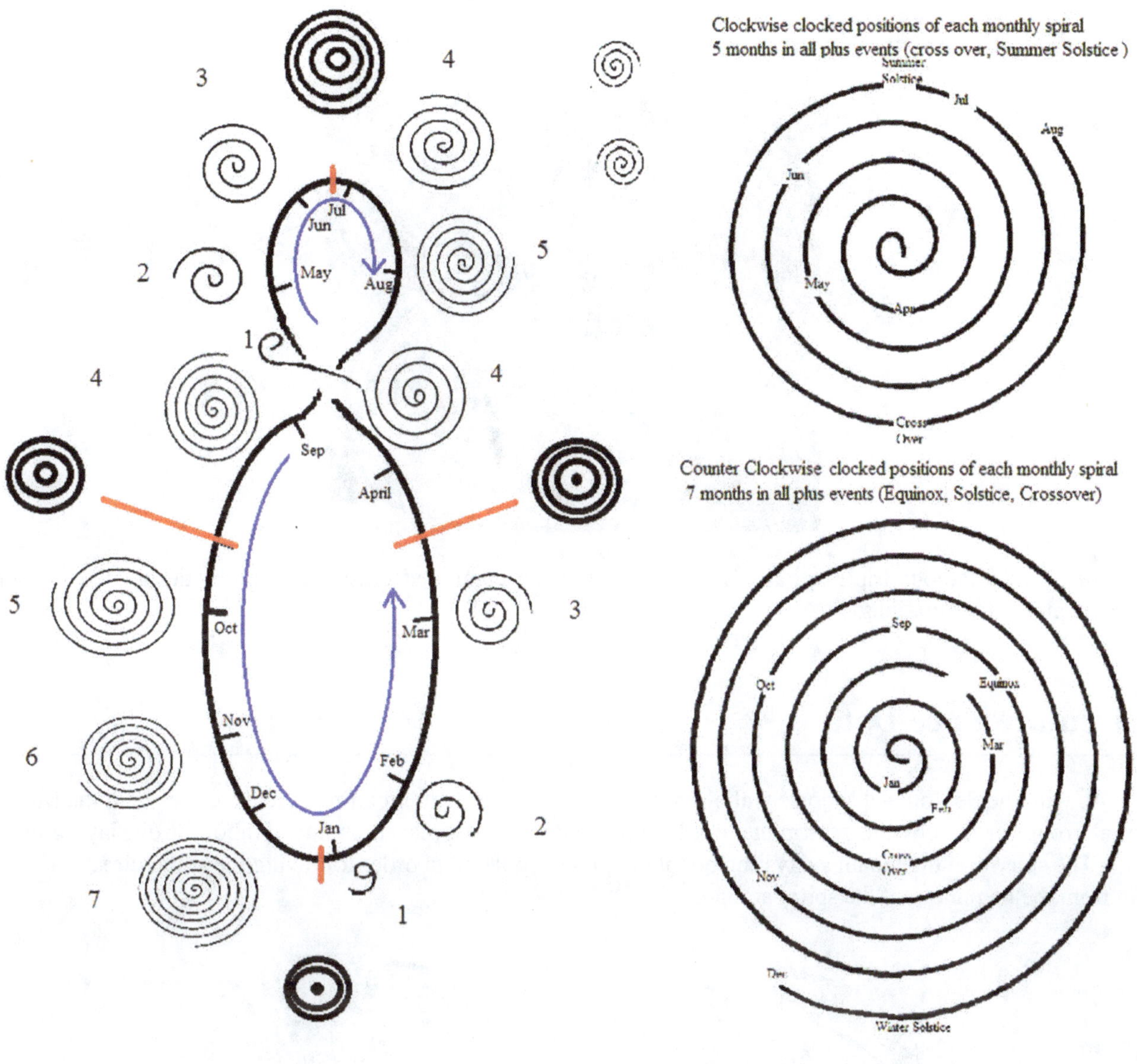

The shadow reverse path of the Sun's figure 8 track
through the sky, called an Analemma.

The months are listed to the inside of the path line of the analemma, the months counting January as 1 thru count upward as indicated by the blue arrow and jump from April to September to continue the counterclockwise direction until December (number 7) is reached. In the top of the figure 8 spiral exists the remaining 5 months from May and ending August.

Crossover

Newgrange famous triple spirals. Enhanced to see the combined crossover months designated in their proper spiral configurations.

Circumference Data

As with the Season and Moon Symbol groups, there are plenty of circumference examples with the Month spiral group for the obvious reason that circumference data can be placed on any symbol for displaying more data. The story thru the month's days can be told in great detail and in order following the spiral direction starting from the beginning of the spiral around.

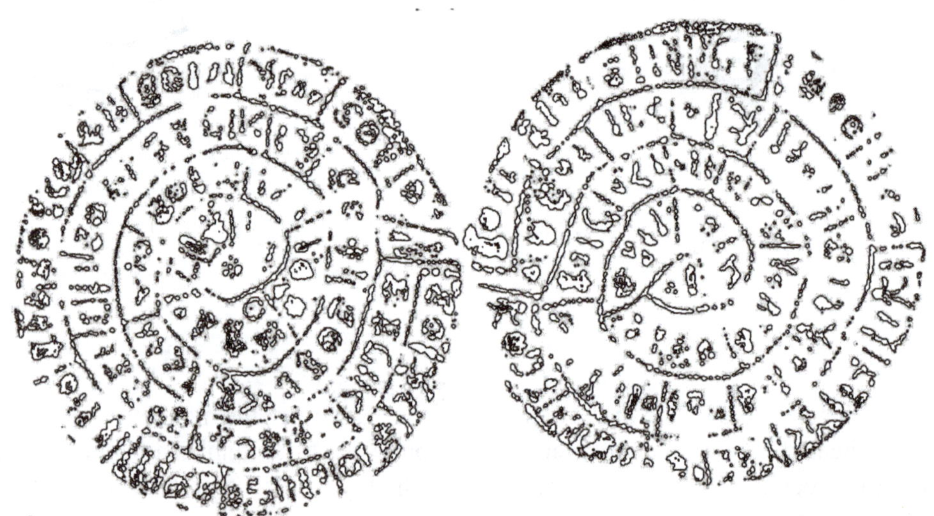

Image by author of stamp of the Phaistos Disc, until me, an undecipherable object. I believed in 2017, as I now know, it is used as a double-sided stamp template created to portray a proper directional stamped image of the entire twelve-month cycle of the year using the shadow spiral analemma symbology of the Ancient Language as a root, with sectioning lines denoting predominantly monthly divisions of the year. I displayed information in my original book denoting specific symbol groups around the outer edge as the month symbols, which was purely to throw off others until I had a chance to decipher the artifact. Which worked as I seen several take up this ruse online, denoting the misled approach. It is a cutthroat world folks.

The site has the largest Season symbol group I've seen, mostly made from the natural rock incorporation in a spectacular display! The images were so large I could not find the **theme** symbol while present at the site, only after I got home and opened up the images I took did I see it! You will see it to the right of the season and in the top image of this story. The theme is always an artistic representation of the object discussed on the panels. Photo of Author

Here is the lines drawn, showing both natural and human made, depicting migration patterns. One of the best representations of rock incorporation, and more importantly, just how much nature seems to provide a story rock already representing the story! The combination of nature to the Universal Language must have relayed a great sense of harmony and symbiosis to the writer to be part of. Tattooing use in this instance could also be said. This symbol of Autumn could include summer? The outlined human shadow lines radiating would determine exactly what dates and combinations exist but such research has not been completely accomplished yet.

Solar Eclipses

The hand with the outstretched fingers is the sign for the Moon blocking the sun! As the very hard to predict event occurred such was recorded in detail, sometimes with paint as people and groups were traveling when it happened. Eclipses can be minor to full and so this information was recorded and transferred to others so knowledge in tracking them could be gained. The type of eclipse coverage was noted on the same panels and any further event data

The main portion of the panel showing hands denoting the solar eclipse events.

Again, beyond bullet holes, the visibly round palm with fingers defining this type of symbol group in event count position one upon the other.

A great example of a round palm with fingers but the palm incorporates the winter solstice and season symbol directly with a 3D count cycle of squared bent fingers (witnessed earlier) from the date of solstice!

The Foot

As the hand is the human symbol to show the moon above the user blocking the light of the sun like the hand would do, there is then an opposite appendage and meaning for the opposite eclipse event seen in nature! The Solar Eclipse and the foot! The foot is the opposite of the hand, which touches and walks upon the earth, which in turn blocks the sun from the moon to create the solar eclipse! In sign the foot can be pointed at or represented with the open hand above the head a fist made with the other hand held against the bottom of the open palm to designate the longer foot form!

These foot and hand opposites are unique and amazingly simple, yet defied anyone from cracking the code do to this simplicity. Just one more way the obvious and easy understanding of UL can be remembered and used forever in the Ancients life! As with the palm being round to represent the moon's circular form and long fingers to represent the hand, the foot has the indignant form of being longer formed with shorter toes to differentiate it from the shorter hand! The form usually has the rounded heel to designate the round earth as well. But as with the lunar eclipse events, the solar eclipse also has various degrees of blocking the suns rays and thus varies accordingly. Remember some foot symbols are not feet at all but pear cactus harvesting with blooming fruit on the tops or loaded burden baskets and both have a different shape and usually has separated or almost separated toes from the main body or the body shape is completely different and they are not associated with any moon or solar/season/monthly symbols!

Another foot symbol Photo and site discovery in Little Colorado River drainage by Dennis Rashay who has photographed many petroglyphs sites.

Ancient Universal Language Root Connection Conclusions

The author has provided ample background information on the ancient language as it relates to the Phaistos Disc and other artifacts. Yet this proof is very limited in this book, so it is suggested to obtain the full field manual Ancient Universal Language of Man (Chris Hegg 2017) at any online location if you the reader is interested in the full spectrum and connection of this language discovered in North America, which is global in usage. Provided here are only excerpts of specific symbols and groups of symbols in relation to the artifact topic.